THE ULTIMATE
CHRISTMAS
COOKBOOK

OVER **200** RECIPES
FOR SEASONAL EATING

THE ULTIMATE
CHRISTMAS
COOKBOOK

OVER **200** RECIPES
FOR SEASONAL EATING

HERMES
HOUSE

First published in 1997 by Hermes House

HERMES HOUSE books are available for bulk purchase for sales
promotion and for premium use. For details, write or call the sales director,
Hermes House, 27 West 20th Street, New York, NY 10011;
(800) 354-9657

Hermes House is an imprint of
Anness Publishing Inc.

ISBN 1-901289-66-4

Publisher: Joanna Lorenz
Project Editor: Sarah Ainley
Photography: Karl Adamson, Steve Baxter, James Duncan, Michelle Garrett,
Amanda Heywood, Don Last & Patrick McLeavey
Recipes: Carla Capalbo, Jacqueline Clark, Carole Clements, Roz Denny, Nicola Diggins,
Joanna Farrow, Christine France, Silvana Franco, Christine Ingram, Judy Jackson,
Elizabeth Lambert Oritz, Wendy Lee, Jane Stevenson, Laura Washburn,
Pamela Westland, Steven Wheeler & Elizabeth Wolf-Cohen
Designer: Siân Keogh

Printed and bound in China

3 5 7 9 10 8 6 4 2

Contents

Introduction 6

Festive Appetizers 14

Main Courses 34

Vegetarian Dishes & Vegetables 60

Buffet Dishes 92

Party Foods 118

Stuffings, Sauces & Preserves 138

Desserts 158

Christmas Baking 194

Christmas Treats & Edible Gifts 220

Festive Drinks & Cocktails 240

Suggested Menus 252

Index 254

$\mathcal{I}$NTRODUCTION

$\mathcal{C}$hristmas is a time for high spirits and good cheer, a time for giving and for sharing. Food plays an essential part in the festive season. The gathering of friends and family around a table laden with rich and lavish fare somehow goes hand in hand with our idea of what Christmas is all about.

While all cooks know the importance of good food at Christmas, they also know that great demands will be made on their time. The secret of a carefree Christmas lies in the planning. Thinking ahead and preparing in advance mean that decision-making under pressure is avoided. As the holidays get closer, the list of things to do gets longer: planning meals and menus, shopping for the freshest and choicest ingredients, followed by all the necessary roasting, chopping, kneading and baking. The preparation of Christmas foods is as much a part of Christmas as the eating and can be just as much fun. Include the whole family by delegating tasks. The excitement mounts as each task is crossed off the list.

This book is packed with inspirational ideas and valuable advice to take Christmas cooks smoothly through the festive season. There are over 200 recipes to choose from, including all the traditional favorites, plus a range of tempting, more unusual dishes that are every bit as festive as the customary fare. The introductory section includes a feature on setting the Christmas scene around the home with beautiful organic decorations. A countdown to Christmas will help you plan your time effectively so that you can ease yourself gently into the holiday season. Also included are professional tips for essential basic techniques such as roasting the turkey, lining a cake pan, and making almond paste and royal icing. A selection of sample menus for the main mealtime events completes the collection and will ensure that every Christmas is a happy and memorable one for the cook and the whole family.

Right: Natural decorations are by far the most beautiful. This easily made garland can be placed on a mantelpiece or used as a door wreath.

Setting the Scene
Evergreen Garland

An evergreen garland, bringing together a host of natural materials, mirrors the beauty of the forest in winter.

MATERIALS

*tape measure • wire-mesh netting •
wire cutters • absorbent florist's-foam,
soaked in water • knife • scissors •
secateurs • stub wires • selection of
evergreens such as pine, holly, ivy,
cypress • bare twigs such as apple and
teasels • dried ferns, sprayed gold
(optional) • large pinecones •
selection of baubles and ribbons*

1 Measure the length of the fireplace
or doorway to be decorated. Cut the
appropriate length of wire-mesh netting
and trim it to a width of 10 inches,
using wire cutters. Cut blocks of
absorbent foam into 6 pieces and place
them end to end along the center of the
netting. Fold over the netting to secure
the foam blocks, and twist the cut edges
together. Measure and mark the center
of the garland length.

2 Decorate the garland with the
evergreens and other natural materials,
pushing the stems under the wire
mesh and into the foam. Continue
adding materials until you reach the
end of the wire cone. Return to the
center of the garland and decorate
outward in the opposite direction.

3 Twist the stub wires around a few
pinecones and push the wires into the
foam at intervals along the garland.

4 Twist the wires around the garland
to hang it securely. Decorate with a
ribbon bow, baubles or large pinecones.

Twig Heart Door Wreath

Welcome seasonal guests with a door wreath that is charming in its simplicity.

MATERIALS

*garden shears • pliable branches
such as buddleia, cut from the garden •
ruler • florist's wire • sea-grass string •
variegated trailing ivy • red berries •
tree ivy • white rose • golden twine*

1 Use garden shears to cut 6 lengths
of pliable branches, 28 inches long.
Wire three branches together at one
end. Repeat with the other three. Cross
the two bundles over at the wired end,
then wire them together in the crossed-
over position.

2 Holding the crossed, wired ends,
ease the long end around and down.
Repeat with the other side to form a
heart shape. Wire the bottom end.

3 Bind the wiring with sea-grass
string and make a hanging loop.

4 Entwine ivy around the heart shape.
Add berries. Make a posy of tree-ivy
leaves and a white rose and tie it with
golden twine. Wire the posy at the top
of the heart shape.

EVERLASTING CHRISTMAS TREE

This delightful little tree, made from dyed, preserved oak leaves and decorated with tiny gilded cones,

makes an enchanting Christmas decoration. Group several together to make a table centerpiece.

MATERIALS

bunch of dried, dark oak leaves •
florist's wire • small pinecones •
picture framer's wax gilt • flowerpot,
7 inches tall • small, dry florist's-foam
cone • knife • 4 florist's stub wires •
large, florist's-foam cone, 7 inches tall

1 Wire up bunches of about four leaves, making separate bunches of large, medium and small leaves.

2 Insert wires into the bottom end of each pinecone and twist the ends together. Gild each cone by rubbing on wax gilt.

3 Prepare the pot by cutting the smaller foam cone to fit, adding stub wires and positioning the larger cone on top. Attach the leaves, starting at the top and working down, to make a realistic shape. Add the gilded cones.

ADVENT CANDLE RING

An advent ring makes a pretty centerpiece. This one uses cinnamon sticks for a rich, sensual aroma.

MATERIALS

florist's-foam • knife •
florist's ring basket • 4 plain white
candles • moss • dried orange slices •
florist's stub wires • garden shears •
cinnamon sticks • golden twine •
tree ivy • physalis

1 Soak the florist's foam and cut it to fit the ring basket. Position the church candles in the foam, then cover the foam with moss, pushing it down at the sides of the basket.

2 Pass stub wire through the center of the orange slices and twist the ends.

3 Wire the cinnamon sticks in bundles, then tie with golden twine and pass a wire through the string. Wire the ivy leaves into bundles.

4 Position the ivy leaves in the ring. Decorate with orange slices and cinnamon sticks, placing the physalis on the candle ring at intervals.

COUNTDOWN TO CHRISTMAS

This at-a-glance timetable will help you plan and organize your Christmas cooking.

If you have chosen your menu from one of those suggested at the back of the book,

the table below suggests when the components may be prepared.

LATE AUTUMN
Make preserves and relishes such as Crab Apple & Lavender Jelly or Christmas Chutney, to serve with cold meats and pies.

NOVEMBER
Second week
Make Moist and Rich Christmas Cake.

Third week
Feed Moist and Rich Christmas Cake.

Fourth week
Make Traditional Christmas Pudding. Plan the Christmas Dinner: consider the number of guests and their food preferences before you plan the menu. Order turkey, goose, beef or ham. Continue to feed Moist and Rich Christmas Cake.

DECEMBER
First week
Make Light Jeweled Fruit Cake.
Make mincemeat for Deluxe Mincemeat Tart.
Continue to feed Moist and Rich Christmas Cake.
Compile complete shopping list for main Christmas meals under headings for different stores or for the various counters at the supermarket.

Second week
Make Almond Paste to cover Moist and Rich Christmas Cake.
Shop for dry goods such as rice, dried fruits and flour.
Order special bread requirements.
Make Cumberland Rum Butter.

Third week
Make Roquefort Tartlets and other pastry-type cocktail savories and freeze them.
Cover Moist and Rich Christmas Cake with royal icing, set aside one day, then cover and store (optional).

Fourth week
Shop for chilled ingredients.
Buy wines and other drinks.

DECEMBER 21
Check thawing time for frozen turkey, duck, beef or other meat.
Large turkeys (25 pounds) need 86 hours (3½ days) to thaw in the refrigerator, or 40 hours at room temperature.
Make a note to take the meat from the freezer at the appropriate time.

DECEMBER 23
Shop for fresh vegetables, if it's not possible to do so on December 24.
Make Cheese and Spinach Tart and freeze (if not making on Christmas Day).
Make Crunchy Apple and Almond tart.

DECEMBER 24
Shop for fresh vegetables, if possible.
Assemble Christmas Salad and refrigerate dressing separately.
Make stuffing for poultry.
Cook poultry giblets to make gravy.
Defrost cocktail pastries.
Prepare bacon rolls by threading them onto toothpicks.

Left: Pottery molds were often used in Victorian times to make decorative Christmas puddings.

CHRISTMAS DAY

This timetable is planned for Christmas Dinner to be served at 2 PM.

If you wish to serve it at a different time, please adjust the times accordingly.

8.30 AM Stuff the poultry. Make stuffing balls with any leftover stuffing, or spoon it into greased ovenproof dishes. Set the table.

9.00 AM Put a steamer or large saucepan on the stove and bring water to a boil. Put the Christmas Pudding on to steam.

TO COOK A 10-POUND TURKEY

9:05 AM Set oven to 425°F.

9:25 AM Put turkey in oven.

9:45 AM Reduce heat to 350°F.
Baste turkey now and at frequent intervals.

12:15 PM Put potatoes around turkey. Remove foil from turkey and baste again.
Turn the potatoes.

12:45 PM Increase heat to 400°F. Put any dishes of stuffing in oven.

1:45 PM Remove turkey and potatoes from oven, put on heated dish, cover with foil and keep warm.
Make gravy and broil bacon rolls.

TO COOK VEGETARIAN MENU

11:15 AM Make pastry for Cheese and Spinach Tart, if not cooking from frozen. (If you are making Christmas Pie, begin 20 minutes earlier to allow time to chill the assembled pie.)

11:45 AM Put pastry in the fridge and chill. Prepare sprouts for Festive Brussels Sprouts.

12:15 PM Preheat oven for Cheese and Spinach Tart.
Remove pastry from fridge and assemble. (For Christmas Pie, chill assembled dish for 20 minutes before baking. Preheat oven 10 minutes before removing pie from fridge.)

1:00 PM Put tart or pie in oven.

1:20 PM Simmer chestnuts for about 10 minutes.

1:30 PM Simmer sprouts for 5 minutes.

1:35 PM Simmer carrots for 5 minutes.

1:40 PM Gently reheat all vegetables together.

1:45 PM Remove tart or pie from oven.

2:00 PM Serve first course.

Above: Bundles of cinnamon sticks are tied together with ribbon for a scented tree trimming. Fresh cranberries are threaded on to sewing thread and fixed to the ribbon, as a complement to the festive colors on the tree.

BASIC TECHNIQUES

CARVING A TURKEY

1 First, remove the leg by cutting the skin between the breast and leg. Press the leg flat, to expose the joint. Cut between the bones through the joint.

2 Cut the leg in two, through the joint.

3 Carve the leg into slices.

4 Remove the wing, cutting through the joint in the same way as for the leg.

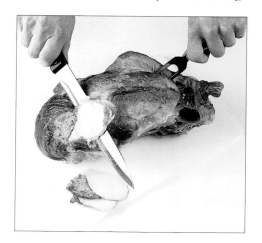

5 Carve the breast in slices, starting at the front of the breast. Carve slices from the back of the breast, alternating the slices between front and back, until all the breast has been carved.

TIMES FOR ROASTING TURKEY

When choosing a turkey for Christmas, you should allow about 1 pound of dressed (plucked and oven-ready) bird per head. A good size turkey to buy for Christmas is 10 pounds. This will serve about 12 people, with leftovers for the following day.

Thaw a frozen turkey, still in its bag, on a plate at room temperature (65–70°F) until the legs are flexible and there are no ice crystals in the cavity of the bird. Remove the giblets from the cavity as soon as the bird has thawed enough.

Oven-ready weight	Thawing time	Number of servings	Cooking time
8 pounds	18 hours	8–10 people	2½–3½ hours
10 pounds	19 hours	12–14 people	3½–4 hours
12 pounds	20 hours	16–18 people	3¾–4½ hours
14 pounds	24 hours	18–20 people	4–5 hours

These times apply to a turkey weighed after stuffing and at room temperature. Cook in a medium oven, 350°F, covered with butter and strips of bacon and loosely covered with foil.

To test whether the turkey is fully cooked, push a skewer into the thickest part of the leg and press the flesh; the juices should run clear and free of any blood. The legs take longer than the breast to cook; keep the breast covered with foil until the legs are cooked. The foil can be removed for the final hour of cooking, to brown and crisp the skin. The turkey should be basted with the juices from the roasting pan every hour of cooking.

Plan for the turkey to be ready 15–20 minutes before you want to serve dinner. Remove it from the oven and let the meat rest before carving it.

ALMOND PASTE

Use almond paste as a base for royal or fondant icing. It will help to keep the cake moist.

INGREDIENTS

*4 cups ground almonds
1 cup superfine sugar
1½ cups confectioners' sugar
1 teaspoon lemon juice
¼ teaspoon almond extract
1 egg*

Makes enough to cover an
8-inch round cake

1 Sift the ground almonds, superfine sugar and confectioners' sugar together in a large mixing bowl.

2 Using a fork, beat the lemon juice, almond extract and egg together in a small bowl. Stir them into the dry ingredients in the mixing bowl until well blended.

3 Knead the paste until smooth. Wrap in plastic wrap until needed.

Royal Icing

INGREDIENTS

2 egg whites
1 teaspoon lemon juice
1 teaspoon glycerin (optional)
1 pound confectioners' sugar

Makes enough to cover an
8-inch round cake

1 In a large bowl, beat the egg whites, lemon juice and glycerin (if using) together with a fork.

2 Sift in enough confectioners' sugar to make a thick paste. Stir to mix.

3 Using a wooden spoon, beat in the remaining confectioners' sugar until the icing forms stiff peaks. Cover with plastic wrap until needed.

Lining a Cake Pan

1 Place the cake pan on a double piece of waxed paper. Draw around the base of the pan and cut out two circles to fit inside the pan.

2 Measure the circumference of the pan with a piece of string and cut a double strip of waxed paper slightly longer than the circumference. Fold over 1 inch along one long side. Cut diagonal slits in the folded-over part, up to the fold line.

3 Grease the pan. Place one circle of paper in the base of the pan. Wrap the double strip around the pan, neatly arranging the snipped edge over the bottom of the pan so it fits flat. Place the second circle of waxed paper on top, to make a smooth base.

Fondant Icing

INGREDIENTS

¼ cup water
1 tablespoon powdered gelatin
2 teaspoons liquid glucose
5 cups confectioners' sugar

Makes enough to cover an
8-inch round cake

1 Put the gelatin in the water in a small bowl and soak for 2 minutes. Place the bowl in a saucepan of hot water and let dissolve over very low heat.

2 Remove the bowl from the hot water and add the glucose to the liquid.

3 Sift the confectioners' sugar into a bowl and add the gelatin mixture. Mix and knead into a paste. Wrap the icing in plastic wrap until needed.

Festive Appetizers

*C*hristmas is all about anticipation: the people you will see, the gifts you will receive and, of course, the Christmas meals you will eat together. A Christmas meal is like a good novel—a tempting beginning that builds to an exciting middle and leads to a satisfying ending. All of the festive appetizers in this chapter will tempt the senses; the trick is to make a good match among the colors, textures and richness of all your courses. Virtually any will complement the traditional turkey, but keep in mind Pumpkin Soup for a beautiful color contrast, or Asian Duck Consommé for an exotic touch. Farmhouse Pâté will balance lighter fish or chicken dishes, while Grilled Brie and Walnuts or Roquefort Tartlets will best suit beef or lamb.

CARROT AND CORIANDER SOUP

Nearly all root vegetables make excellent soups, as they purée well and have an earthy flavor that

complements the sharper flavors of herbs and spices, and carrots are particularly versatile.

This simple soup is elegant in both flavor and appearance.

INGREDIENTS

1 pound carrots, preferably young and
tender
1 tablespoon sunflower oil
3 tablespoons butter
1 onion, chopped
1 celery stalk, plus 2–3 pale leafy celery
tops
2 small potatoes, chopped
4 cups chicken stock
2–3 teaspoons ground coriander
1 tablespoon chopped fresh cilantro
1 cup milk
salt and freshly ground black pepper

Serves 4–6

1 Trim the carrots, peel if necessary and cut into chunks. Heat the oil and 2 tablespoons of the butter in a large flameproof casserole or heavy saucepan and fry the onion over low heat for 3–4 minutes, until slightly softened but not browned.

2 Slice the celery stalk crosswise. Add the celery and potatoes to the onion in the pan, cook for a few minutes and then add the carrots. Fry over low heat for 3–4 minutes, stirring, and then cover. Reduce the heat and sweat for 10 minutes. Shake the pan occasionally so that the vegetables do not stick.

3 Add the stock, bring to a boil and then partially cover and simmer for another 8–10 minutes, or until the carrots and potatoes are tender.

4 Remove 6–8 tiny celery leaves for use as a garnish and finely chop the remaining celery tops (about 1 tablespoon when chopped). Melt the remaining butter in a small saucepan and fry the ground coriander for about 1 minute, stirring constantly.

5 Reduce the heat, add the finely chopped celery and fresh cilantro and fry over low heat for about 1 minute. Set aside.

6 Process the soup in a food processor or blender until smooth and pour into a clean saucepan. Stir in the milk, coriander mixture and seasoning. Heat gently, taste and adjust the seasoning as necessary. Serve the soup garnished with the reserved celery leaves.

COOK'S TIP

For a more piquant flavor,
add a little lemon juice to the soup
just before serving.

CREAM OF MUSHROOM SOUP

A good mushroom soup makes the most of the subtle and sometimes rather elusive flavor of mushrooms.

Button mushrooms are used here for their pale color; portobello mushrooms give

a fuller flavor but will turn the soup a darker shade of brown.

INGREDIENTS

3¾ cups button mushrooms
1 tablespoon sunflower oil
3 tablespoons butter
1 small onion, finely chopped
1 tablespoon flour
1¼ cups vegetable stock
1¾ cups milk
pinch of dried basil
2–3 tablespoons light cream (optional)
fresh basil leaves, to garnish
salt and freshly ground black pepper

Serves 4

1 Pull the mushroom caps away from the stalks. Finely slice the caps and finely chop the stalks, keeping the two piles separate.

2 Heat the sunflower oil and half the butter in a heavy saucepan and add the chopped onion, mushroom stalks and one-half of the sliced mushroom caps. Fry for 1–2 minutes, stirring frequently, then cover and sweat over low heat for 6–7 minutes, stirring occasionally.

3 Stir in the flour and cook for about 1 minute. Gradually add the stock and milk to make a smooth, thin sauce. Add the basil, and season with salt and pepper. Bring to a boil and then simmer, partly covered, for 15 minutes.

4 Let the soup cool slightly and then pour into a food processor or blender and process until smooth. Melt the remaining butter in a heavy frying pan, and fry the remaining mushrooms over low heat for 3–4 minutes, or until they are just tender.

5 Pour the soup into a large, clean saucepan and stir in the sliced mushrooms. Heat until very hot but not boiling and add salt and ground black pepper to taste. Add a little of the light cream, if using. Ladle the soup into four warmed bowls and serve immediately, sprinkled with the fresh basil leaves.

Pumpkin Soup

The sweet flavor of pumpkin is good in soups, teaming well with other more savory

ingredients such as potatoes to make a warm and comforting dish.

INGREDIENTS

1 tablespoon sunflower oil
2 tablespoons butter
1 large onion, sliced
large wedge (about 1½ pounds) pumpkin
1 pound potatoes, sliced
2½ cups vegetable stock
generous pinch of nutmeg
1 teaspoon chopped fresh tarragon
2½ cups milk
1–2 teaspoons lemon juice
salt and freshly ground black pepper

Serves 4–6

1 Heat the sunflower oil and butter in a frying pan and fry the onion for 4–5 minutes. Stir frequently.

2 Transfer the onion to a saucepan and add the pumpkin and potato. Stir well, then cover with the lid and sweat over low heat for about 10 minutes, until the vegetables are almost tender. Stir the vegetables occasionally to prevent them from sticking to the pan.

3 Stir in the stock, nutmeg, tarragon and seasoning. Bring the liquid to a boil and then simmer for about 10 minutes, or until the vegetables are completely tender.

4 Let the liquid cool slightly away from the heat, then pour into a food processor or blender and process until smooth. Pour back into a clean saucepan and add the milk. Heat gently and then taste, adding the lemon juice and extra seasoning if necessary. Serve piping hot with crusty brown rolls.

COOK'S TIP

Pumpkins are readily available in supermarkets throughout the winter months. Other colorful vegetables, such as squashes, can also be used to make tempting Christmas soups.

Asian Duck Consommé

Christmas need not be about just traditional European flavors. This soup is both light

and rich at the same time and has intriguing flavors of Southeast Asia.

INGREDIENTS

*1 duck carcass (raw or cooked), plus
2 legs or any giblets, trimmed of fat
1 large onion, unpeeled, with root end
trimmed
2 carrots, cut into 2-inch pieces
1 parsnip, cut into 2-inch pieces
1 leek, cut into 2-inch pieces
2–4 garlic cloves, crushed
1-inch piece fresh ginger, peeled and
sliced
1 tablespoon black peppercorns
4–6 thyme sprigs, or 1 teaspoon dried thyme
6–8 fresh cilantro sprigs, leaves and stems
separated*

For the Garnish
*1 small carrot
1 small leek, halved lengthwise
4–6 shiitake mushrooms, thinly sliced
soy sauce
2 scallions, thinly sliced
watercress or shredded Chinese cabbage
freshly ground black pepper*

Serves 4

1 Put the duck carcass, with the legs or giblets, the onion, carrots, parsnip, leek and garlic in a large saucepan or flameproof casserole. Add the ginger, peppercorns, thyme and cilantro stems, cover with cold water and bring to a boil over medium-high heat. Skim off any foam on the surface.

2 Reduce the heat and simmer gently for 1½–2 hours, then strain through a cheesecloth-lined sieve into a bowl, discarding the bones and vegetables. Cool the stock and chill for several hours or overnight. Skim off any congealed fat and carefully blot the surface with paper towels to remove any traces of fat.

3 For the garnish, cut the carrot and leek into 2-inch pieces and then lengthwise into thin slices. Stack and slice into thin julienne strips. Place in a saucepan with the mushrooms. Pour in the stock and add a few dashes of soy sauce and some pepper.

4 Bring to a boil over medium heat, skimming off any foam that rises to the surface. Adjust the seasoning. Stir in the scallions and watercress or shredded Chinese cabbage. Serve the consommé sprinkled with the cilantro leaves.

Warm Shrimp Salad with Spicy Marinade

Most of the ingredients for this salad can be prepared in advance, but wait until just before serving to cook the shrimp and bacon. Spoon them onto the salad and serve with hot herb-and-garlic bread.

Ingredients

1 pound large, cooked, shelled shrimp, about 25
8 ounces bacon, chopped
mixed lettuce leaves, washed and dried
2 tablespoons snipped fresh chives

For the Lemon and Chili Marinade
1 garlic clove, crushed
finely grated rind of 1 lemon
1 tablespoon lemon juice
¼ cup olive oil
¼ teaspoon chili paste, or a large pinch dried ground chili
1 tablespoon light soy sauce
salt and freshly ground black pepper

Serves 8

1 In a glass bowl, mix the shrimp with the garlic, lemon rind and juice, 3 tablespoons oil, the chili paste and soy sauce. Season with salt and pepper. Cover with plastic wrap and marinate for at least one hour.

2 Gently cook the bacon in the remaining oil until crisp. Drain well.

3 Tear the lettuce into bite-size pieces and arrange on plates.

4 Just before serving, put the shrimp with their marinade in a frying pan, bring to a boil, add the bacon and cook for one minute. Spoon onto the lettuce and sprinkle with snipped chives.

SMOKED SALMON SALAD

This recipe works equally well using smoked trout instead of salmon. The dressing can be made in

advance and stored in the fridge until you are ready to eat.

INGREDIENTS

4 thin slices white bread
oil, for frying
paprika, for dusting
mixed salad greens
1 ounce Parmesan cheese
8 ounces smoked salmon, thinly sliced
1 lemon, cut into wedges

For the Vinaigrette
6 tablespoons olive oil
2 tablespoons red wine vinegar
1 garlic clove, crushed
1 teaspoon Dijon mustard
1 teaspoon honey
1 tablespoon chopped fresh parsley
½ teaspoon fresh thyme
2 teaspoons capers, chopped
salt and freshly ground black pepper

Serves 8

1 First, make the dressing. Put all the ingredients in a screw-top jar and shake the jar well. Season to taste.

2 With a small star-shaped cutter, stamp out shapes from the bread. Heat 1 inch oil in a shallow frying pan until the oil is almost smoking (test it with a cube of bread; it should sizzle on the surface and brown within 30 seconds). Fry the croutons in batches until golden brown. Remove the croutons and drain on paper towels. Dust with paprika and let cool.

3 Wash the lettuce, dry the leaves and tear them into small bite-size pieces. Wrap the leaves in a clean, damp dishcloth and keep the lettuce in the fridge until ready to serve.

4 Shave the Parmesan cheese into wafer-thin flakes with a vegetable peeler. Put the flakes in a dish and cover with plastic wrap.

5 Cut the salmon into ½-inch strips no more than 2 inches long.

6 Arrange the lettuce on individual plates. Scatter the Parmesan over the lettuce and arrange the salmon strips on top. Shake the dressing vigorously again and spoon onto the salad. Scatter the croutons on top and place a lemon wedge on the side of each plate.

CHRISTMAS SALAD

A light and simple first course that can be prepared ahead and assembled just before serving.

INGREDIENTS

Mixed red and green lettuce leaves
2 sweet pink grapefruit
1 large or 2 small avocados, peeled and cubed

For the Dressing
6 tablespoons olive oil
2 tablespoons red wine vinegar
1 garlic clove, crushed
1 teaspoon Dijon mustard
salt and freshly ground black pepper

For the Caramelized Orange Peel
4 oranges
¼ cup superfine sugar
¼ cup cold water

Serves 8

1 For the caramelized peel, using a vegetable peeler, remove the rind from the oranges in thin strips and reserve the fruit. Scrape the white pith from the rind with a sharp knife, and cut the rind in fine shreds.

2 Put the sugar and water in a small pan and heat gently until the sugar has dissolved. Then, add the shreds of orange rind, increase the heat and boil steadily for 5 minutes, until the rind is tender. Using two forks, remove the orange rind from the syrup and spread it out on a wire rack to dry. (This can be done the day before.) Reserve the syrup to add to the dressing.

3 Wash and dry the lettuce and tear the leaves into bite-size pieces. Wrap them in a damp dishcloth and chill. Over a bowl, cut the oranges and grapefruit into segments, removing the pith.

4 Put the dressing ingredients into a screw-top jar and shake vigorously to emulsify the dressing. Add the reserved orange-flavored syrup and adjust the seasoning to taste. Arrange the salad ingredients on individual plates with the avocados, spoon on the dressing and scatter the caramelized peel on top.

WILD MUSHROOM POLENTA

The wild mushrooms used here have a wonderful flavor and texture, which combine well

with polenta to make an unusual appetizer or light snack.

INGREDIENTS

1 pound small new potatoes
5½ cups light vegetable stock
6 ounces baby carrots, trimmed and peeled
6 ounces sugar snap peas
4 tablespoons (½ stick) unsalted butter
3 ounces oyster mushrooms, trimmed and sliced
5 shiitake mushrooms, fresh or dried, chopped
1½ cups fine polenta or cornmeal
2 shallots or 1 small onion, chopped
2 fist-size pieces of cauliflower
4 ounces chanterelle mushrooms, trimmed and sliced
⅔ cup light cream or half-and-half
3 egg yolks
2 teaspoons lemon juice
salt and cayenne pepper

Serves 4

1 Lightly oil an 8-cup loaf pan and line with a sheet of waxed paper. Set aside. Put the potatoes in a pan, cover with boiling water, add a pinch of salt and cook for 20 minutes. Bring the vegetable stock to a boil, add the carrots and sugar snaps and cook for 3–4 minutes. Remove the vegetables with a slotted spoon and keep warm. Add 2 tablespoons of the butter and all of the oyster and shiitake mushrooms to the stock and simmer for 5 minutes.

2 Pour the polenta into the saucepan in a steady stream and stir for 2–3 minutes, or until thickened. Transfer the polenta to the prepared pan, cover and let become firm.

3 For the sauce, melt the remaining butter, add the shallots and cook gently. Cut the cauliflower into bite-size pieces, add to the pan with the chanterelles, and cook for 2–3 minutes. Add the cream and the reserved cooked vegetables and simmer to eliminate any moisture.

4 Remove from the heat, stir in the egg yolks and let residual heat slightly thicken the sauce. The sauce must not boil at this stage. Add the lemon juice, then season with salt and a dash of cayenne pepper.

5 To serve, turn the warm polenta out onto a board, slice with a wet knife and arrange on four warmed serving plates. Spoon the mushroom and vegetable sauce over the polenta. If preferred, the polenta loaf can be prepared in advance and stored in the freezer.

GOAT CHEESE SOUFFLÉ

Make sure everyone is seated before the soufflé comes out of the oven, because it will begin to deflate almost immediately. This recipe works equally well with strong blue cheeses such as Roquefort.

INGREDIENTS

2 tablespoons butter
2 tablespoons flour
¾ cup milk
1 bay leaf
freshly grated nutmeg
grated Parmesan cheese, for sprinkling
1½ ounces herb-and-garlic soft cheese
5 ounces aged goat cheese, diced
6 egg whites, at room temperature
¼ teaspoon cream of tartar
salt and freshly ground black pepper

Serves 4–6

1 Melt the butter in a heavy saucepan. Add the flour and cook, stirring, until golden. Pour in half the milk, stirring vigorously until smooth, then stir in the remaining milk and add the bay leaf. Season with a pinch of salt and plenty of pepper and nutmeg. Reduce the heat, cover and simmer for about 5 minutes, stirring occasionally.

2 Preheat the oven to 375°F. Generously butter a 6-cup soufflé dish and sprinkle with Parmesan cheese.

3 Remove the sauce from the heat and discard the bay leaf. Stir in both cheeses until melted.

4 In a clean, grease-free bowl, using an electric mixer or balloon whisk, beat the egg whites slowly until they become frothy. Add the cream of tartar, increase the speed and continue beating, until they form soft peaks, then stiffer peaks.

5 Stir a spoonful of beaten egg white into the cheese sauce to lighten it, then pour the cheese sauce over the remaining whites. Using a metal spoon, gently fold the sauce into the whites until the mixtures are just combined, cutting down to the bottom, then along the side of the bowl and up to the top.

6 Gently pour the soufflé mixture into the prepared dish and bake for 25–30 minutes, or until puffed and golden brown. Serve immediately.

BROILED BRIE AND WALNUTS

This unusual cheese recipe will impress your guests, since it looks as though it has been made

professionally. You'll be pleased to know that it requires almost no preparation.

INGREDIENTS

1 tablespoon butter, at room temperature
1 teaspoon Dijon mustard
1½-pound wheel of Brie or
Camembert cheese
¼ cup chopped walnuts
1 loaf French bread, sliced and
toasted, to serve

Serves 16–20

2 Sprinkle the surface with the walnuts and broil for 2–3 more minutes, or until the nuts are golden. Serve immediately with the French-bread toasts. Let your guests help themselves, as the whole grilled Brie makes an attractive centerpiece.

1 Preheat the broiler. In a small bowl, cream the butter and Dijon mustard, and spread evenly over the surface of the cheese. Transfer the cheese to a flameproof serving plate, and broil 4–6 inches from the heat for 3–4 minutes, or until the top just begins to bubble.

ROQUEFORT AND CUCUMBER MOUSSE

This refreshingly cool mousse makes a perfect appetizer to prepare ahead and store in

the fridge. If you prefer, other blue-veined French cheeses, such as Bleu d'Auvergne

or Fourme d'Ambert, may be used instead of Roquefort.

INGREDIENTS

1 small cucumber (6–8 inches long)
½ envelope (2 teaspoons) powdered gelatin
5 tablespoons cold water
3½ ounces Roquefort cheese
1 package (8 ounces) cream cheese
3 tablespoons crème fraîche or sour cream
cayenne or white pepper
seedless red and green grapes and fresh
mint leaves, to garnish

Serves 6

1 Using a sharp kitchen knife, cut the cucumber lengthwise into quarters. Remove the seeds and cut the cucumber strips into 1-inch pieces. Chop the cucumber pieces finely.

2 Sprinkle the gelatin over the cold water in a small heatproof bowl. Let the gelatin stand to soften for about 2 minutes, then place the bowl in a shallow pan of simmering water. Heat until the gelatin is dissolved, stirring occasionally.

3 In a mixing bowl (or in a food processor fitted with a metal blade), mix both types of cheese with the crème fraîche until smooth. Add the dissolved gelatin and blend. Add the chopped cucumber to the bowl, mixing well without reducing the cucumber to a purée. Season to taste with cayenne.

4 Rinse a 6-cup dish or mold with cold water to prevent the mousse from sticking to it when removed. Carefully spoon the mixture into the dish or mold and tap gently to remove air bubbles. Chill for 4–6 hours or overnight, until well set.

5 To remove, run a knife around the edge of the dish or mold, dip in hot water for 10–15 seconds and wipe the wet base. Place a large plate over the top of the dish and invert both together, shaking firmly to release the mousse. Garnish with the grapes and fresh mint leaves.

COOK'S TIP

Its delicate taste and elegant appearance make this mousse a great addition to any buffet supper or party menu.

PÂTÉ DE FOIE GRAS IN FILO CUPS

This is an extravagantly rich hors d'oeuvre, so it is perfect for special occasions such as Christmas Day.

Any other fine liver pâté may be used if foie gras is unavailable.

INGREDIENTS

3–6 fresh or defrosted sheets filo pastry
3 tablespoons butter, melted
8 ounces canned foie gras or other fine
liver pâté, at room temperature
4 tablespoons (½ stick) butter, softened
2–3 tablespoons cognac or brandy
(optional)
chopped pistachios, to garnish

Makes about 24

COOK'S TIP

The pâté and pastry are best eaten soon after preparation. If preparing ahead and refrigerating, be sure to bring back to room temperature before serving.

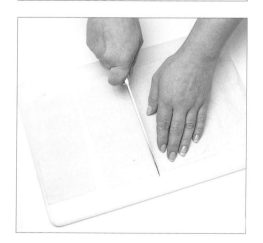

1 Preheat the over to 400°F. Grease a muffin pan with 1½-inch cups. Stack the filo sheets on a work surface and cut into 2½-inch squares. Cover with a damp towel to prevent the pastry from drying out.

2 Keeping the rest of the filo squares covered, place one square on a work surface and brush lightly with melted butter, then turn over and brush the other side. Butter a second square and place it over the first at an angle. Butter a third square and place at a different angle over the first two sheets to form an uneven edge.

3 Press the pastry layers into the cups of the muffin pan. Continue with the remaining pastry and butter until all the cups are filled.

4 Bake the filo cups for 4–6 minutes, until crisp and golden, then let cool in the pan for 5 minutes. Carefully remove each filo cup to a wire rack and cool completely.

5 In a small bowl, beat the pâté with the softened butter until smooth and well blended. Add the cognac or brandy to taste, if using. Spoon into a piping bag fitted with a medium star nozzle and pipe a swirl into each cup. Sprinkle with pistachios. Refrigerate until ready to serve.

CHICKEN LIVER MOUSSE

This mousse makes an elegant yet easy first course. The onion marmalade makes a delicious

accompaniment, along with a salad of chicory or other bitter greens.

INGREDIENTS

1 pound chicken livers
12 tablespoons butter (1½ sticks), diced
1 small onion, finely chopped
1 garlic clove, finely chopped
½ teaspoon dried thyme
2–3 tablespoons brandy
salt and freshly ground black pepper
green salad, to serve

For the Onion Marmalade
2 tablespoons butter
1 pound red onions, thinly sliced
1 garlic clove, finely chopped
½ teaspoon dried thyme
2–3 tablespoons red wine vinegar
1–2 tablespoons honey
¼ cup golden raisins

Serves 6–8

1 Use a sharp knife to trim the chicken livers, cutting off any green spots and removing any filaments or fat.

2 In a heavy frying pan, melt 2 tablespoons of the butter. Add the finely chopped onion and cook for 5–7 minutes over low heat, until soft and golden, then add the garlic to the pan and cook for 1 more minute. Increase the heat and add the chicken livers, thyme, salt and freshly ground black pepper. Cook for 3–5 minutes, until the livers are colored, stirring frequently; the livers should remain pink inside, but not raw. Add the brandy, stirring, and cook for one more minute.

3 Using a slotted spoon, transfer the livers to a food processor fitted with a metal blade. Pour in the cooking juices and process for 1 minute or until smooth, scraping down the sides once. With the machine running, add the remaining butter, a few pieces at a time, until it is incorporated.

4 Press the mousse mixture through a fine sieve with a wooden spoon or rubber spatula until it has a creamy, smooth consistency.

5 Line a 6-cup loaf pan with plastic wrap, smoothing out as many wrinkles as possible. Pour the mousse mixture into the lined pan. Cool, then cover and chill until firm.

6 To make the onion marmalade, heat the butter in a frying pan, add the onions and cook for 20 minutes, until softened and just colored. Stir in the chopped garlic, thyme, vinegar, honey and golden raisins and cook, covered, for 10–15 minutes, stirring occasionally, until the onions are completely soft and jam-like. Spoon into a serving bowl and let cool to room temperature.

7 To serve, dip the loaf pan into hot water for 5 seconds, wipe dry and invert. Lift off the pan, peel off the plastic wrap and smooth the surface with a spatula. Serve sliced, with the onion marmalade and a green salad.

FARMHOUSE PÂTÉ

This pâté is full of flavor and can be cut into slices for easy serving. You can make it in

ramekin dishes or in a larger container, if you are expecting an unspecified number of guests.

INGREDIENTS

8 bacon strips
2 boneless chicken breast halves
8 ounces chicken livers
1 onion, chopped
1 garlic clove, crushed
½ teaspoon salt
½ teaspoon freshly ground black pepper
1 teaspoon anchovy paste
1 teaspoon ground mace
1 tablespoon chopped fresh oregano
1 cup fresh white bread crumbs
1 egg
2 tablespoons brandy
⅔ cup chicken stock
½ envelope (2 teaspoons) gelatin

To Garnish
strips of pimiento and black olives

Makes 1 pound

1 Preheat the oven to 325°F. Press the bacon slices flat with a knife to stretch them slightly. Line the base and sides of each dish with bacon and neatly trim any excess off the edges.

2 Place the chicken breasts and livers, onion and garlic in a food processor. Process until smooth. Add the salt, pepper, anchovy paste, mace, oregano, bread crumbs, egg and brandy. Process until smooth.

3 Divide the mixture among the dishes. Cover the dishes with a double thickness of foil and stand them in a roasting pan. Add enough hot water to come halfway up the sides of the pan.

4 Bake in the center of the oven for 1 hour, or until firm. Remove the foil to release the steam. Place a weight on top of each dish to flatten until cool.

5 Pour the juices from each dish into a measuring cup and add chicken stock to make ⅔ cup. Heat in a pan until boiling. Blend the gelatin with 2 tablespoons water and pour into the stock, stirring until dissolved. Let cool.

6 Garnish the pâté when cold, then spoon the gelatin mixture over the top. Chill until set. Cover with plastic wrap.

BAKED EGGS WITH CREAMY LEEKS

This recipe can also be prepared using other vegetables, such as puréed spinach

or ratatouille, as a base. For such an elegant dish, it needs very little preparation time.

INGREDIENTS

*1 tablespoon butter, plus extra for
greasing
8 ounces small leeks, thinly sliced
5–6 tablespoons whipping cream
freshly grated nutmeg
4 eggs
salt and freshly ground black pepper*

Serves 4

1 Preheat the oven to 375°F. Generously butter the base and sides of four ramekins or individual soufflé dishes.

2 Melt the butter in a small frying pan and cook the leeks over medium heat, stirring frequently, until softened but not browned.

3 Add 3 tablespoons of the whipping cream and cook over low heat for about 5 minutes, or until the leeks are very soft and the cream has thickened a little. Add plenty of salt, freshly ground black pepper and nutmeg to the frying pan, to season.

4 Arrange the ramekins or soufflé dishes in a small roasting pan and divide the leeks among them. Break an egg into each, spoon 1–2 teaspoons of the remaining cream over each egg and season lightly.

5 Pour boiling water into the baking dish to come halfway up the sides of the ramekins or soufflé dishes. Bake for about 10 minutes, or until the egg whites are set and the yolks are still quite soft, or a little longer if you prefer your eggs more well cooked.

ROQUEFORT TARTLETS

These can be made in shallow tart pans to serve hot as a first course. You could also make them

in a muffin pan with tiny cups, to serve warm as bite-size snacks with a drink before a meal.

INGREDIENTS

1½ cups all-purpose flour
large pinch of salt
8 tablespoons (1 stick) butter
1 egg yolk
2 tablespoons cold water

For the Filling
1 tablespoon butter
1 tablespoon flour
⅔ cup milk
4 ounces Roquefort cheese, crumbled
⅔ cup heavy cream
½ teaspoon dried mixed herbs
3 egg yolks
salt and freshly ground black pepper

Makes 12

1 To make the pastry, sift the flour and salt into a large mixing bowl and rub the butter into the flour until it resembles bread crumbs. Mix the egg yolk with the water and stir into the flour to make a soft dough. Knead until smooth, wrap in plastic wrap and chill for 30 minutes.

2 For the filling melt the butter, and stir in the flour and the milk. Boil to thicken, stirring continuously. Off the heat, beat in the cheese and season. Let cool. Bring the cream and herbs to a boil. Reduce the mixture to 2 tablespoons. Beat into the sauce with the egg yolks.

3 Preheat the oven to 375°F. On a lightly floured work surface, roll out the pastry ⅛ inch thick. Stamp out rounds with a fluted cutter and use to line the tartlet pans.

4 Divide the filling among the tartlets so each one is two-thirds full. Stamp out smaller fluted rounds or star shapes and lay on top of each tartlet. Bake for 20–25 minutes, or until golden brown.

Main Courses

*F*or purists, there can be no other main course than
Roast Turkey on Christmas Day, but an equally festive
main dish of pheasant, goose or duck will provide such
an attractive centerpiece that even traditionalists at the
table won't object. And who's to say that the seasonal
celebration can't be marked with a seafood dish such
as Lobster Thermidor or Sea Bass with Citrus Fruit?
Of course, venison, lamb and pork tenderloin all have their
own appeal, so the choice may be a difficult one. If you're
having a big crowd for dinner, try making several main
dishes, such as Roast Beef with Roasted Sweet Peppers and
Chicken with Morels, and see which has less left over afterward.

ROAST GOOSE WITH CARAMELIZED APPLES

Choose a young goose with a pliable breast bone for the best possible flavor.

INGREDIENTS

*1 goose (10–12 pounds), with giblets
(thawed overnight, if frozen)
salt and freshly ground black pepper*

For the Apple and Nut Stuffing
*2 cups prunes
⅔ cup port or red wine
1½ pounds apples, peeled, cored and
cubed
1 large onion, chopped
4 celery stalks, sliced
1 tablespoon mixed dried herbs
finely grated rind of 1 orange
goose liver, chopped
1 pound pork sausagemeat
1 cup chopped pecans
2 eggs*

For the Caramelized Apples
*4 tablespoons (½ stick) butter
¼ cup red currant jelly
2 tablespoons red wine vinegar
8 small apples, peeled and cored*

For the Gravy
*2 tablespoons all-purpose flour
2½ cups giblet stock
juice of 1 orange*

Serves 8

1 The day before cooking the goose, soak the prunes in the port. After the soaking time, remove each prune from the marinade, pit each one and cut it into four pieces. Reserve the port and prunes separately and set aside.

2 The next day, mix the prunes with all the remaining stuffing ingredients and season well. Moisten with half the reserved port.

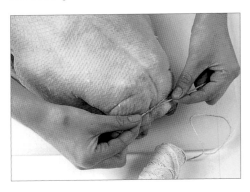

3 Preheat the oven to 400°F. Stuff the neck end of the goose, tucking the flap of skin under and securing it with a small skewer. Remove the excess fat from the cavity and pack the cavity with the stuffing. Tie the legs together to hold them in place.

4 Weigh the stuffed goose to calculate the cooking time: allow 15 minutes per 1 pound. Put the bird on a rack in a roasting pan and rub the skin with salt. Prick the skin all over to help the fat run out. Roast for 30 minutes, then reduce the heat to 350°F and roast for the remaining cooking time. Pour off any fat produced during cooking into a bowl. The goose is cooked when the juices run clear when the thickest part of the thigh is pierced with a skewer. Pour a little cold water over the breast to crisp the skin.

5 Meanwhile, prepare the caramelized apples. Melt the butter, red currant jelly and vinegar in a small roasting pan or a shallow ovenproof dish. Put in the apples, baste them well and bake for 15–20 minutes. Baste the apples halfway through the cooking time. Do not cover them or they will collapse.

6 Lift the goose onto the serving dish and let it stand for 15 minutes before carving. Pour off the excess fat from the roasting pan, leaving any sediment in the bottom. Stir in the flour, cook gently until brown, and then blend in the stock. Bring to a boil, and add the remaining reserved port, orange juice and seasoning. Simmer for 2–3 minutes. Strain into a gravy boat. Surround the goose with the caramelized apples and spoon the red currant glaze on top.

ROAST TURKEY

Serve this classic Christmas roast with stuffing balls, bacon rolls, roast potatoes, Brussels sprouts and gravy.

INGREDIENTS

1 oven-ready turkey (10 pounds), with
giblets (thawed, if frozen)
1 large onion, peeled and studded with
6 whole cloves
4 tablespoons (½ stick) butter, softened
10 sausages
salt and freshly ground black pepper

For the Stuffing
8 ounces bacon, chopped
1 large onion, finely chopped
1 pound pork sausage
⅓ cup rolled oats
2 tablespoons chopped fresh parsley
2 teaspoons dried mixed herbs
1 large egg, beaten
4 ounces dried apricots, finely chopped

For the Gravy
2 tablespoons flour
2 cups giblet stock

Serves 8

1 Preheat the oven to 400°F. Adjust the spacing of the shelves to allow for the size of the turkey. To make the stuffing, cook the bacon and the chopped onion together over low heat in a heavy frying pan until the bacon is crisp and the onion is tender but not browned. Transfer the cooked bacon and onion to a large mixing bowl and add all the remaining stuffing ingredients. Season with plenty of salt and freshly ground black pepper and mix well to blend.

2 Stuff the neck end of the turkey only, tucking the flap of skin under and securing it with a small skewer or stitching it in place with thread. Do not overstuff the turkey, or the skin will burst during cooking. Reserve any remaining stuffing and set aside.

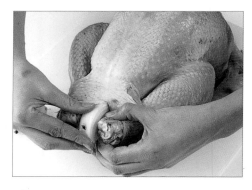

3 Put the onion studded with cloves in the body cavity of the turkey and tie the legs together with string to hold them in place. Weigh the stuffed bird and calculate the cooking time: Allow 15 minutes per pound plus 15 minutes extra. Place the turkey in a large roasting pan.

4 Brush the turkey with the butter and season well with salt and pepper. Cover it loosely with foil and cook it for 30 minutes. Baste the turkey with the pan juices, then lower the oven temperature to 350°F and cook for the remainder of the calculated time. Baste the turkey every 30 minutes or so.

5 With wet hands, shape the remaining stuffing into small balls or pack it into a greased ovenproof dish. Bake for 20 minutes, or until golden brown and crisp. About 20 minutes before the end of cooking, put the chipolata sausages in an ovenproof dish and put them in the oven. Remove the foil from the turkey for the last hour of cooking and baste. The turkey is cooked when the juices run clear when the thickest part of the thigh is pierced with a skewer.

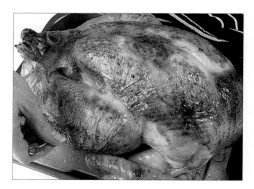

6 Transfer the turkey to a serving plate, cover it with foil and let it stand for 15 minutes before carving. Spoon off the fat from the roasting pan, leaving the meat juices. Blend in the flour and cook for 2 minutes. Gradually stir in the stock and bring to a boil. Check the seasoning and pour into a sauceboat. Remove the skewer from the turkey neck and pour any juices into the gravy. To serve, surround the turkey with chipolata sausages, bacon rolls and stuffing.

ROAST PHEASANT WITH PORT

Roasting the pheasant in foil helps to keep the flesh particularly moist and succulent. This recipe

is best for very young birds and, if you have an obliging butcher, you should

request the more tender female birds.

INGREDIENTS

vegetable oil
2 oven-ready pheasants,
about 1½ pounds each
4 tablespoons (½ stick) butter, softened
8 fresh thyme sprigs
2 bay leaves
6 bacon strips
1 tablespoon flour
¾ cup chicken stock
1 tablespoon red currant jelly
3–4 tablespoons port
freshly ground black pepper

Serves 4

1 Preheat the oven to 450°F. Line a large roasting pan with a sheet of strong foil large enough to enclose both of the pheasants. Lightly brush the foil with vegetable oil.

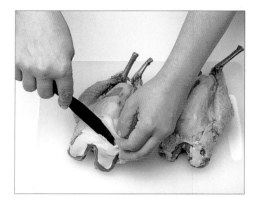

2 Wipe the pheasants with damp paper towels and remove any extra fat or skin. Using your fingertips, carefully loosen the skin of the breasts. With a round-bladed knife or small spatula, spread the butter between the skin and the breast meat of each bird. Tie the legs securely with string, then lay the thyme sprigs and a bay leaf over the breast of each bird.

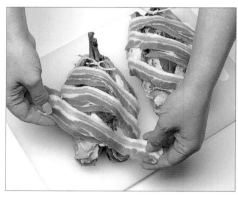

3 Lay bacon strips over the breasts, place the birds in the foil-lined pan and season with plenty of ground black pepper. Bring together the long ends of the foil, fold over securely to enclose, then twist firmly together to seal.

4 Roast the birds for 20 minutes, then reduce the oven temperature to 375°F and cook for another 40 minutes. Uncover the birds and roast 10–15 more minutes, or until they are browned and the juices run clear when the thigh of each of the birds is pierced with a skewer. Transfer the birds to a board and let stand, covered with clean foil, for 10 minutes before carving.

5 Pour the juices from the foil into the roasting pan and skim off any fat. Sprinkle the flour over the juices and cook over medium heat, stirring continuously, until the mixture is smooth. Whisk in the stock and the red currant jelly and bring to a boil. Simmer until the sauce thickens slightly, adding more stock if needed, then stir in the port and adjust the seasoning to taste. Strain the sauce and serve immediately, with the pheasants.

VARIATION

Other game birds that would be suitable for this type of cooking include guinea fowl and partridge.

CHICKEN WITH RED WINE VINEGAR

These chicken breasts with their slightly tart taste make an original, light and tasty Christmas meal. You could substitute tarragon vinegar, if desired.

INGREDIENTS

4 chicken breast halves (about 7 ounces each), skinned and boned
4 tablespoons (½ stick) unsalted butter
freshly ground black pepper
8–12 shallots, trimmed and halved
¼ cup red wine vinegar
2 garlic cloves, finely chopped
¼ cup dry white wine
½ cup chicken stock
1 tablespoon chopped fresh parsley
green salad, to serve

Serves 4

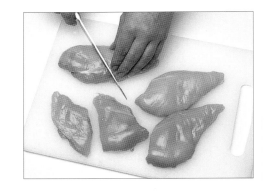

1 Using a sharp kitchen knife, cut each chicken breast half in half horizontally to make eight pieces.

2 Melf half the butter in a heavy frying pan over medium heat. Add the chicken and cook for 3–5 minutes, until golden brown, turning once, then season with pepper.

3 Add the shallot halves to the pan, cover and cook over low heat for 5–7 minutes, shaking the pan and stirring the pieces occasionally.

4 Transfer the chicken pieces to a plate. Add the vinegar and cook, stirring frequently, for about 1 minute, until the liquid is almost evaporated. Add the garlic, wine and stock and stir.

5 Return the chicken to the pan with any accumulated liquid. Cover and simmer for 2–3 minutes, until the chicken is tender and the juices run clear when the meat is pierced with a knife or skewer.

6 Transfer the chicken and the shallots to a serving dish and cover to keep warm. Increase the heat and rapidly boil the cooking liquid until it has reduced by half.

7 Off the heat, gradually add the remaining butter, whisking until the sauce is slightly thickened and glossy. Stir in the parsley and pour the sauce over the chicken pieces and shallots. Serve immediately with a green salad.

CHICKEN WITH MORELS

Morels are delicious dried mushrooms. Although they're expensive, a little goes a long way.

Use fresh morels (about 10 ounces), if you prefer, or chanterelle, shiitake or oyster mushrooms.

INGREDIENTS

1½ ounces dried morel mushrooms
1 cup chicken stock
4 tablespoons (½ stick) butter
5 or 6 shallots, thinly sliced
4 ounces button mushrooms, sliced
¼ teaspoon dried thyme
¾ cup heavy cream
¾ cup brandy
4 chicken breast halves (about 7 ounces each), skinned and boned
1 tablespoon vegetable oil
¾ cup champagne or dry sparkling white wine
salt and freshly ground black pepper

Serves 4

1 Put the morels in a strainer and rinse well under cold running water, shaking to remove as much sand as possible. Put them in a large heavy saucepan with the stock and bring to a boil over medium-high heat. Remove the pan from the heat and let stand for 1 hour.

2 Remove the morels from the cooking liquid and strain the liquid through a very fine sieve or cheesecloth-lined strainer; reserve for the sauce. Reserve a few whole morels and slice the rest.

3 Melt half the butter in a frying pan over medium heat. Add the shallots and cook for 2 minutes, until softened, then add the morels and mushrooms and cook, stirring frequently, for 2–3 minutes. Season well with salt and ground black pepper and add the thyme, ⅓ cup of cream and the brandy. Reduce the heat and simmer for 10–12 minutes, until any liquid has evaporated, stirring occasionally. Remove the morel mixture from the frying pan and set aside.

4 Pull off the fillets from the chicken breasts. (The fillet is the finger-shaped piece on the underside of the breast.) Wrap the fillets tightly in plastic wrap and freeze, to reserve for another use. Make a pocket in each chicken breast by cutting a slit with a sharp knife along the thicker edge, taking care not to cut all the way through the meat.

5 Using a small spoon, fill each pocket with one-quarter of the mushroom mixture, then close and, if necessary, secure with a toothpick to hold the stuffing inside the chicken.

6 Melt the remaining butter with the oil in a frying pan over medium heat and cook the chicken breasts on one side for 6–8 minutes. Transfer to a plate. Add the champagne to the pan and boil to reduce by half. Add the strained morel cooking liquid and boil to reduce by half again.

7 Add the remaining cream and cook over medium heat for 2–3 minutes, until the sauce thickens and coats the back of a spoon. Season. Return the chicken to the pan with any juices and the reserved whole morels, and simmer for 3–5 minutes over medium-low heat, until the juices run clear when the meat is pierced with a skewer.

DUCK WITH ORANGE SAUCE

Commercially raised ducks tend to have more fat than wild ducks. In this recipe, the initial slow cooking

and pricking the skin of the duck help to draw out the excess fat.

INGREDIENTS

1 duck, about 4½ pounds
2 oranges
½ cup superfine sugar
6 tablespoons white wine vinegar or cider
vinegar
½ cup Grand Marnier or other orange
liqueur
salt and freshly ground black pepper
watercress and orange slices, to garnish

Serves 2–3

1 Preheat the oven to 300°F. Trim off all the excess fat and skin from the duck and prick the skin all over with a fork. Generously season the duck inside and out with salt and freshly ground black pepper, and tie the legs together with string to hold them in place.

2 Place the duck on a rack in a large roasting pan. Cover tightly with foil and cook for 1½ hours. Using a vegetable peeler, remove the rind in wide strips from the oranges, then stack up two or three strips at a time and slice into very thin julienne strips. Squeeze the juice from the oranges and set it aside.

3 Place the sugar and vinegar in a small heavy saucepan and stir to dissolve the sugar. Boil over high heat, without stirring, until the mixture is a rich caramel color. Remove the pan from the heat and, standing back, carefully add the freshly squeezed orange juice, pouring it down the side of the pan. Swirl the pan to blend, then bring back to a boil and add the orange rind and liqueur. Simmer for 2–3 minutes.

4 Remove the duck from the oven and pour off all the fat from the roasting pan. Raise the oven temperature to 400°F.

5 Roast the duck, uncovered, for 25–30 minutes, basting three or four times with the caramel mixture, until the duck is golden brown and the juices run clear when the thigh is pierced with a skewer.

6 Pour the juices from the cavity into the saucepan and transfer the duck to a carving board. Cover loosely with foil and let stand for 10–15 minutes. Pour the roasting juices into the saucepan with the remaining caramel mixture, skim the fat and simmer gently. Serve the duck with the orange sauce, garnished with sprigs of watercress and orange slices.

ROAST LEG OF VENISON

The marinade for this recipe forms the base for a deliciously tangy, slightly sweet sauce that

perfectly complements the richness of roasted venison.

INGREDIENTS

1 onion, chopped
1 carrot, chopped
1 celery stalk, chopped
3 or 4 garlic cloves, crushed
4–6 fresh parsley sprigs
4–6 fresh thyme sprigs
2 bay leaves
1 tablespoon peppercorns, lightly crushed
3 cups red wine
¼ cup vegetable oil, plus more for brushing
1 young venison haunch (about 6 pounds), trimmed
2 tablespoons flour
1 cup beef stock
1 unwaxed orange
1 unwaxed lemon
¼ cup red currant or raspberry jelly
¼ cup ruby port or Madeira
1 tablespoon cornstarch, blended with 2 tablespoons water
1 tablespoon red wine vinegar
fresh herbs, to garnish

Serves 6–8

1 Place the onion, carrot, celery, garlic, parsley, thyme, bay leaves, peppercorns, wine and oil in a dish large enough to hold the venison, then add the venison and turn to coat. Cover the dish with plastic wrap and let marinate in the fridge for 2–3 days, turning occasionally.

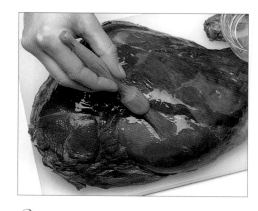

2 Preheat the oven to 350°F. Remove the meat from its marinade and pour the marinade into a saucepan. Pat the meat dry, then brush with a little oil and wrap in foil.

3 Roast the venison for 15–20 minutes per pound for rare to medium meat. About 25 minutes before the end of the cooking time, remove the foil, sprinkle the venison with the flour and baste.

4 Add the stock to the marinade and boil until reduced by half, then strain and set aside.

5 Using a vegetable peeler, remove the rind from the orange and half the lemon. Cut the pieces into thin julienne strips. Bring a saucepan of water to a boil and add the orange and lemon strips. Simmer them for 5 minutes, then drain and rinse under cold water.

6 Squeeze the juice of the orange into a medium saucepan. Add the red currant jelly and cook over low heat until melted, then stir in the port and the reduced marinade and simmer gently for 10 minutes, stirring.

7 Stir the blended cornstarch mixture into the marinade and cook, stirring frequently, until the sauce is slightly thickened. Add the vinegar and the orange and lemon strips and simmer for another 2–3 minutes. Keep warm, stirring occasionally to keep the fruit strips separated.

8 Transfer the venison to a board and let stand, loosely covered with foil, for 10 minutes before carving. Garnish with your chosen fresh herbs and serve with the sauce.

FILET MIGNON WITH MUSHROOMS

This haute cuisine French dish was originally made with truffle slices, but large mushroom caps

are less expensive and look just as attractive, especially when they are fluted.

INGREDIENTS

4 thin slices white bread
*4 ounces pâté de foie gras or mousse de
foie gras*
4 large mushroom caps
5 tablespoons butter
2 teaspoons vegetable oil
4 fillet steaks, each about 1 inch thick
3–4 tablespoons Madeira or port
½ cup beef stock
watercress, to garnish

Serves 4

1 Cut the bread into rounds about the same diameter as the steaks, using a large round cutter or by cutting into squares, then cutting off the corners. Toast the bread and spread with the foie gras, dividing it evenly. Place the bread on warmed plates.

2 Flute the mushroom caps using the edge of a knife blade. Melt about 1 tablespoon of the butter and sauté the mushrooms until golden. Transfer the mushrooms to a plate and keep warm.

3 In the same pan, melt another 1 tablespoon of the butter with the oil, swirling to combine. When the butter just begins to brown, add the steaks and cook for 6–8 minutes, turning once, until cooked as desired (medium-rare meat will still be slightly soft when pressed, medium will be springy and well-done firm). Place the steaks on the bread and top with the cooked mushroom caps.

4 Add the Madeira to the pan and boil for 20–30 seconds. Add the stock and boil until reduced by three-quarters. Swirl in the remaining butter. Pour a little sauce over each steak, then garnish with sprigs of watercress.

CHATEAUBRIAND WITH BÉARNAISE SAUCE

Chateaubriand is a lean and tender cut of beef from the thick center of the fillet that is

pounded to give it its characteristic shape. This portion is for two people and

would be perfect for a romantic Christmas meal à deux.

INGREDIENTS

10 tablespoons (1¼ sticks) butter,
cut into pieces
1½ tablespoons tarragon vinegar
1½ tablespoons dry white wine
1 shallot, finely chopped
2 egg yolks
1 pound beef fillet (5–6 inches long), cut
from the thickest part of the fillet
1 tablespoon vegetable oil
salt and freshly ground black pepper
Sautéed Potatoes, to serve

Serves 2

1 Clarify the butter by melting in a saucepan over low heat; do not boil. Skim off any foam and set aside.

2 Put the vinegar, wine and shallot in a small heavy saucepan over high heat and boil to reduce until the liquid has almost evaporated. Remove from the heat and cool slightly. Add the egg yolks and whisk for 1 minute. Place the saucepan over very low heat and whisk constantly until the yolk mixture begins to thicken and the whisk begins to leave tracks on the base of the pan, then remove the pan from the heat.

3 Whisk in the butter, slowly at first, then more quickly, until the sauce thickens. Season and keep warm.

4 Place the meat between two sheets of waxed paper or plastic wrap and pound with the flat side of a meat pounder or roll with a rolling pin to flatten to about 1½ inches thick. Season with plenty of salt and pepper.

5 Heat the vegetable oil in a heavy frying pan over medium-high heat. Add the meat and cook for 10–12 minutes, turning once, until cooked as desired (medium-rare meat will be slightly soft when pressed, medium will be springy and well-done will be firm).

6 Transfer the steak to a board and, using a very sharp kitchen knife, carve into thin, diagonal slices. If you want a smooth sauce, strain it through a fine sieve, then serve with the steak, accompanied by Sautéed Potatoes.

ROAST BEEF WITH ROASTED BELL PEPPERS

This substantial and warming dish makes an ideal dinner for cold winter nights.

INGREDIENTS

1 sirloin steak 3–3½ pounds
1 tablespoon olive oil
8 small red bell peppers
¾ cup mushrooms
6 ounces thickly sliced pancetta, cubed
2 tablespoons flour
⅔ cup full-bodied red wine
1¼ cups beef stock
2 tablespoons marsala
2 teaspoons mixed dried herbs
salt and freshly ground black pepper

Serves 8

1 Preheat the oven to 375°F. Season the meat. Heat the oil in a pan, then brown the meat. Place in a roasting pan and cook for 1¼ hours.

2 Put the red bell peppers in the oven to roast for 20 minutes (or roast for 45 minutes if using larger peppers).

3 Near the end of the meat's cooking time, prepare the gravy. Roughly chop the mushroom caps and stems.

4 Heat the pan again and add the pancetta. Cook until the fat runs from the meat. Add the flour to the pan and cook for a few minutes, until browned.

5 Stir in the red wine and stock and bring to a boil. Lower the heat and add the marsala, herbs and seasoning.

6 Add the mushrooms and heat through. Remove the sirloin from the oven and let stand for 10 minutes. Serve with the peppers and hot gravy.

ROAST STUFFED LAMB

This lamb is stuffed with a tempting blend of kidneys, spinach and rice.

INGREDIENTS

*boneless leg or shoulder of lamb
(4–4½ pounds), not tied
2 tablespoons butter, softened
1–2 tablespoons flour
½ cup white wine
1 cup chicken or beef stock
salt and freshly ground black pepper
watercress, to garnish
Sautéed Potatoes, to serve*

For the Stuffing
*5 tablespoons butter
1 small onion, finely chopped
1 garlic clove, finely chopped
⅓ cup long-grain rice
⅔ cup chicken stock
½ teaspoon dried thyme
4 lamb kidneys, halved and cored
10 ounces young spinach leaves, well
washed
salt and freshly ground black pepper*

Serves 6–8

1 To make the stuffing, melt
2 tablespoons of the butter in a
saucepan over medium heat. Add the
onion and cook for 2–3 minutes, until
just softened, then add the garlic and
rice and cook for 1–2 minutes, stirring
constantly, until the rice appears
translucent. Add the stock, salt and
pepper and thyme and bring to a boil,
stirring occasionally, then reduce the
heat and cook, covered, for about 18
minutes, until the rice is tender and the
liquid is absorbed. Transfer the rice into
a bowl and fluff with a fork.

2 In a frying pan, melt 2 tablespoons
of the remaining butter over medium-
high heat. Add the kidneys and cook
for 2–3 minutes, turning once, until
lightly browned but still pink inside,
then transfer to a board and let cool.
Cut the kidneys into pieces and add to
the rice, season with salt and pepper
and toss to combine.

3 In a frying pan, heat the remaining
butter over medium heat until
foaming. Add the spinach leaves and
cook for 1–2 minutes, until wilted,
drain off excess liquid, then transfer
the leaves to a plate and let cool.

4 Preheat the oven to 375°F. Lay
the meat skin side down on a work
surface and season with salt and
pepper. Spread the spinach leaves in
an even layer over the surface, then
spread the stuffing in an even layer
over the spinach. Roll up the meat
like a jelly roll and use a skewer to
close the seam. Tie the meat at 1-inch
intervals to hold its shape, then place
in a roasting pan, spread with the
butter and season.

5 Roast for 1½–2 hours, until the juices
run slightly pink when pierced with
a skewer or until a meat thermometer
inserted into the thickest part of the
meat registers 135–140°F (for medium-
rare to medium). Transfer the meat to a
carving board, cover with foil and let sit
for about 20 minutes.

6 Skim off the fat from the roasting pan.
Place the pan over medium heat and
bring to a boil. Sprinkle on the flour and
cook for 3 minutes, until browned,
stirring and scraping the base of the pan.
Whisk in the wine and stock and bring
to a boil. Cook for 5 minutes, until the
sauce thickens. Season and strain.
Garnish the meat with watercress and
serve with the gravy and potatoes.

BAKED HAM WITH CUMBERLAND SAUCE

Serve this delicious cooked meat and sauce either hot or cold.

INGREDIENTS

1 ham (5 pounds), smoked or unsmoked
1 onion
1 carrot
1 celery stalk
1 bouquet garni
6 peppercorns
whole cloves

For the Glaze
¼ cup light brown sugar
2 tablespoons light corn syrup
1 teaspoon English mustard powder

For the Cumberland Sauce
juice and shredded rind of 1 orange
2 tablespoons lemon juice
½ cup port or red wine
¼ cup red currant jelly

Serves 8–10

1 Soak the ham overnight in a cool place in enough cold water to cover. Discard this water. Put the ham in a large pan and cover it with more cold water. Bring the water to a boil slowly and skim off any scum that rises to the surface.

2 Add the vegetables and seasonings, cover the pan and simmer over low heat for 2 hours.

3 Let the meat cool in the liquid for 30 minutes. Then remove it from the liquid and strip off the skin neatly with the help of a knife (use rubber gloves if the ham is too hot).

4 Score the fat into diamonds with a sharp knife and stick a clove in the center of each diamond.

5 Preheat the oven to 350°F. Put the sugar, corn syrup and mustard powder in a small pan and heat gently to melt them. Place the ham in a roasting pan and spoon the glaze over it. Bake it until golden brown, about 20 minutes. Put it under a hot broiler, if necessary, to get a good color. Let stand in a warm place for 15 minutes before carving.

6 For the sauce, put the orange and lemon juice in a pan with the port and jelly, and heat to melt the jelly. Pour boiling water over the orange rind, drain, and add to the sauce. Cook for 2 minutes. Serve in a sauceboat.

TENDERLOIN OF PORK WRAPPED IN BACON

This easy-to-carve dish is served with an onion and prune gravy.

INGREDIENTS

*3 large pork fillets, about
2½ pounds total
8 ounces bacon
2 tablespoons (¼ stick) butter
⅔ cup red wine*

*For the Prune Stuffing
2 tablespoons (¼ stick) butter
1 onion, very finely chopped
4 ounces mushrooms, finely chopped
4 ready-to-eat prunes, pitted and chopped
2 teaspoons mixed dried herbs
2 cups fresh white bread crumbs
1 egg
salt and freshly ground black pepper*

*To Finish
16 pitted prunes
⅔ cup red wine
16 pickling onions
2 tablespoons flour
1¼ cups chicken stock*

Serves 8

3 Stretch each bacon strip with the back of a large knife.

4 Overlap the strips across the meat. Cut lengths of string and lay them at ¾-inch intervals over the bacon. Cover with a piece of foil, hold in place and roll the pork over. Fold the bacon over the meat and tie the string to secure it. Roll the pork back onto the bacon seams and remove the foil.

5 Place in a roasting pan and spread the butter over the pork. Pour the wine around the meat and cook for 1¼ hours, basting occasionally with the liquid in the roasting pan, until evenly browned. Simmer the remaining prunes in the red wine until tender. Boil the onions in salted water for 10 minutes, or until just tender. Drain and add to the prunes.

6 Transfer the pork to a serving plate, remove the string, cover loosely with foil and let stand for 10–15 minutes before carving into slices. Remove any fat from the roasting pan, add the flour to the sediment and juices and cook gently for 2–3 minutes. Then blend in the stock, bring to a boil and simmer for 5 minutes. Adjust the seasoning to taste. Strain the gravy over the prunes and onions, reheat and serve in a sauceboat with a ladle.

1 Preheat the oven to 350°F. Trim the fillets, removing any sinew and fat. Cut each fillet lengthwise three-quarters of the way through, open them out and flatten.

2 For the stuffing, melt the butter, cook the onion until tender, add the mushrooms and cook for 5 minutes. Transfer to a bowl and mix in the remaining stuffing ingredients. Spread the stuffing over two of the fillets and sandwich together with the third fillet.

Sea Bass with Citrus Fruit

Try this recipe using fresh sea bass for friends or family who would appreciate an

alternative to meat or poultry at Christmastime; it would be an ideal choice for

a New Year's Eve dinner. The delicate flavor of the fish is complemented

perfectly by the citrus fruits and olive oil.

INGREDIENTS

1 small grapefruit
1 orange
1 lemon
1 sea bass (about 3 pounds), cleaned and scaled
6 fresh basil sprigs
flour, for dusting
3 tablespoons olive oil
4–6 shallots, peeled and halved
¼ cup dry white wine
1 tablespoon butter
salt and freshly ground black pepper
fresh dill, to garnish

Serves 6

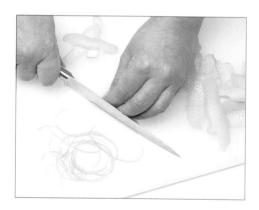

1 With a vegetable peeler, remove the rind from the grapefruit, orange and lemon. Cut into julienne strips, cover and set aside. Peel off the white pith from the fruits and, working over a bowl to catch the juices, cut out the segments from the grapefruit and orange and set them aside for the garnish. Slice the lemon thickly.

2 Preheat the oven to 375°F. Wipe the fish dry inside and out and season the cavity with salt and pepper. Make three diagonal slashes on each side. Reserve a few basil sprigs for the garnish and fill the cavity with the remaining basil, the lemon slices and half the julienne strips of citrus rind.

3 Dust the fish lightly with flour. In a roasting pan or flameproof casserole large enough to hold the fish, heat 2 tablespoons of the olive oil over medium-high heat and cook the fish for about 1 minute, until the skin just crisps and browns on one side. Add the halved shallots to the roasting pan.

4 Place the fish in the preheated oven and bake for about 15 minutes, then carefully turn the fish over and stir the shallots. Drizzle the fish with the remaining oil and bake for another 10–15 minutes, until the flesh is opaque throughout.

5 Carefully transfer the fish to a heated serving dish and remove and discard the cavity stuffing. Pour off any excess oil and add the wine and 2–3 tablespoons of the fruit juices to the pan. Bring to a boil over high heat, stirring. Stir in the remaining julienne strips of citrus rind and boil for 2–3 minutes, then whisk in the butter. Spoon the shallots and sauce around the fish and garnish with fresh dill and the reserved basil and grapefruit and orange segments.

VARIATION
When sea bass is not available, a whole gray mullet or large trout would make a good alternative.

SOLE WITH SHRIMP AND MUSSELS

This luxurious dish is a classic seafood recipe. It is a true feast for fish lovers at any time

of the year and would make a welcome change at Christmas.

INGREDIENTS

6 tablespoons (¾ stick) butter
8 shallots, finely chopped
1¼ cups dry white wine
2¼ pounds mussels, scrubbed and
debearded
8 ounces button mushrooms, quartered
1 cup fish stock
12 skinless lemon or Dover sole fillets,
3–5 ounces each
2 tablespoons flour
¼ cup crème fraîche or heavy cream
½ pound (about 20) cooked, peeled
medium shrimp
salt and white pepper
fresh parsley sprigs, to garnish

Serves 6

2 Transfer the mussels to a large bowl. Strain the mussel cooking liquid through a cheesecloth-lined sieve and set aside. When cool enough to handle, reserve a few mussels in their shells for the garnish. Then, remove the rest from their shells and set aside, covered.

4 Melt the remaining butter in a small saucepan over medium heat. Add the flour and cook for 1–2 minutes, stirring constantly; do not let the flour mixture brown. Gradually whisk in the reduced fish cooking liquid, and the reserved mussel liquid, pour in any liquid from the fish, then bring to a boil, stirring constantly.

1 In a large, heavy flameproof casserole, melt 1 tablespoon of the butter over medium-high heat. Add half the shallots and cook, stirring frequently, for about 2 minutes, until they are softened but not browned. Add the white wine and bring to a boil, then add the mussels and cover tightly. Cook the mussels over high heat, shaking and tossing the pan occasionally, for 4–5 minutes, until the shells open. Discard any mussels that do not open.

3 Melt half the remaining butter in a large, heavy frying pan over medium heat. Add the remaining shallots and cook, stirring frequently, for 2 minutes, or until just softened. Add the mushrooms and fish stock and bring just to the simmering point. Season the fish fillets with salt and pepper. Fold or roll them and slide gently into the stock. Cover and poach for 5–7 minutes, or until the flesh is opaque. Transfer the fillets to a warmed serving dish and cover tightly to keep warm. Increase the heat and boil the liquid until it has reduced by one-third.

5 Reduce the heat to medium-low and cook the sauce for 5–7 minutes, stirring frequently. Whisk in the crème fraîche and keep stirring over low heat until the sauce is well blended. Adjust the seasoning to taste, then add the reserved mussels and the cooked shrimp to the sauce. Cook gently for 2–3 minutes to heat through, then spoon the sauce over the fish and serve garnished with fresh parsley sprigs and the mussels in their shells.

Lobster Thermidor

Lobster thermidor is a rich and delicious dish that is luxurious enough

to serve at Christmas. Serve one lobster per person as a main course or

one filled shell each for an appetizer.

INGREDIENTS

2 live lobsters, about 1½ pounds each
1½ tablespoons butter
2 tablespoons flour
2 tablespoons brandy
½ cup milk
6 tablespoons whipping cream
1 tablespoon Dijon mustard
lemon juice, salt and white pepper
grated Parmesan cheese, for sprinkling
fresh parsley and dill, to garnish

Serves 2–4

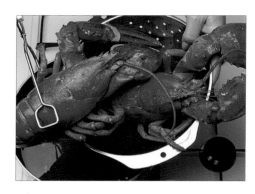

1 Boil the lobsters in a large saucepan of salted water for 8–10 minutes.

2 Cut the lobsters in half lengthwise and discard the dark sac behind the eyes, then pull out the stringlike intestine from the tail. Remove the meat from the shells, reserving the coral and liver, then rinse the shells thoroughly under running water and wipe dry. Cut the meat into bite-size pieces.

3 Melt the butter in a heavy saucepan over medium-high heat. Stir in the flour and cook, stirring, until slightly golden. Pour in the brandy and milk, whisking vigorously until smooth, then whisk in the cream and mustard.

4 Push the lobster coral and liver through a sieve into the sauce and whisk briskly to blend. Reduce the heat to low and simmer gently for about 10 minutes, stirring frequently, until thickened. Season the sauce with salt, if needed, then add pepper and lemon juice.

5 Preheat the broiler. Arrange the lobster shells in a gratin dish or shallow flameproof baking dish.

6 Stir the lobster meat into the sauce and divide the mixture evenly among the shells. Sprinkle with Parmesan cheese and broil until golden. Serve piping hot, garnished with fresh herbs.

SALMON STEAKS WITH SORREL SAUCE

Salmon and sorrel are a traditional combination—the sharp flavor of the sorrel balances the richness

of the fish. If sorrel is not available, use finely chopped watercress instead.

INGREDIENTS

2 salmon steaks, about 8 ounces each
1 teaspoon olive oil
1 tablespoon butter
2 shallots, finely chopped
3 tablespoons whipping cream
4 ounces fresh sorrel leaves, washed and patted dry
salt and freshly ground black pepper
fresh sage, to garnish

Serves 2

1 Season the salmon steaks with salt and freshly ground black pepper. Brush a nonstick frying pan with oil.

2 Place the frying pan over medium heat until hot. Add the salmon steaks and cook for about 5 minutes, until the flesh is opaque next to the bone. If you're not sure, pierce with the tip of a sharp knife; the juices should run clear.

3 Meanwhile, in a small saucepan, melt the butter over medium heat and fry the shallots, stirring frequently, until just softened. Add the cream and the sorrel to the shallots and cook, stirring constantly, until the sorrel is completely wilted. Arrange the salmon steaks on two warmed plates, garnish with fresh sage and serve immediately, with the sorrel sauce.

COOK'S TIP

If preferred, cook the salmon steaks in a microwave oven for 4–5 minutes, tightly covered, or according to the manufacturer's guidelines.

Vegetarian Dishes & Vegetables

*I*n any Christmas celebration nowadays, it's likely that you'll have some vegetarian guests, and they'll appreciate more than just the leftover vegetables. Many recipes here, such as Vegetarian Christmas Pie or Cheese, Rice and Vegetable Strudel, can stand alone as vegetarian main courses or will make a wonderful accompaniment to the turkey in place of traditional vegetables and potatoes. There is a strong ethnic element in vegetarian cooking, and Pumpkin Gnocchi or Spiced Vegetable Couscous will bring an international flavor to the Christmas table. And what would Christmas be without Brussels sprouts, parsnips and potatoes, all cooked in ways to make them extra special?

VEGETARIAN CHRISTMAS PIE

A sophisticated mushroom tart a cheese-soufflé topping. Serve hot with cranberry relish

and Brussels sprouts with chestnuts and carrots.

INGREDIENTS

2 cups flour
¾ cup butter
2 teaspoons paprika
4 ounces Parmesan cheese, grated
1 egg, beaten with 1 tablespoon cold water
1 tablespoon Dijon mustard

For the Filling
2 tablespoons butter
1 onion, finely chopped
1–2 garlic cloves, crushed
5 cups mushrooms, chopped
2 teaspoons mixed dried herbs
1 tablespoon chopped fresh parsley
1 cup fresh white bread crumbs
salt and freshly ground black pepper

For the Cheese Topping
2 tablespoons butter
2 tablespoons flour
1¼ cups milk
1 ounce Parmesan cheese, grated
3 ounces Cheddar cheese, grated
¼ teaspoon English mustard powder
1 egg, separated

Serves 8

1 To make the pastry, sift the flour into a bowl and rub in the butter until the mixture resembles fine bread crumbs. Stir in the paprika and the Parmesan cheese. Bind to a soft pliable dough with the egg and water. Knead until smooth, wrap in plastic wrap and chill for 30 minutes.

2 For the filling, melt the butter and cook the onion until tender. Add the garlic and mushrooms and cook, uncovered, for 5 minutes, stirring occasionally. Increase the heat and pour off any liquid in the pan. Remove the pan from the heat and stir in the dried herbs, parsley, bread crumbs and seasoning. Let cool.

3 Preheat the oven to 375°F. Put a baking sheet in the oven. On a lightly floured surface, roll out the pastry and use it to line a 9-inch loose-bottomed tart pan, pressing the pastry into the edges and making a narrow rim around the top edge. Chill for 20 minutes.

4 For the cheese topping, melt the butter in a pan, stir in the flour and cook for 2 minutes. Gradually blend in the milk. Bring to a boil to thicken, and simmer for 2–3 minutes. Remove the pan from the heat and stir in the cheeses, mustard powder and egg yolk, and season well. Beat until smooth. Whisk the egg white until it holds soft peaks. Then, using a metal spoon, fold the egg white into the topping.

5 To assemble the pie, spread the Dijon mustard evenly over the base of the pastry shell with a spatula. Spoon in the mushroom filling and level the surface by tapping the shell firmly on the work surface.

6 Pour the topping over the filling and bake the pie on the hot baking sheet for 35–45 minutes, until the topping is golden. The pastry shell should sound hollow when tapped on the bottom. Serve immediately or freeze.

VEGETABLE GNOCCHI

This delicious vegetarian main course can be assembled well ahead of time—always a bonus at Christmas.

INGREDIENTS

1 pound frozen spinach
1 tablespoon butter
¼ teaspoon grated nutmeg
1 cup ricotta or cottage cheese
1 cup grated Parmesan cheese
2 eggs, beaten
1 cup flour
½ cup grated Cheddar cheese
salt and freshly ground black pepper

For the Sauce
4 tablespoons (½ stick) butter
¼ cup flour
2½ cups milk

For the Vegetable Layer
2 tablespoons butter
2 leeks or onions, sliced
4 carrots, sliced
4 celery stalks, sliced
4 small zucchini, sliced

Serves 8

1 Put the spinach in a large saucepan with the butter and heat gently to defrost it. Using a wooden spoon, carefully break up the spinach to help it thaw out, then increase the heat to pour off any moisture. Season well with salt, freshly ground black pepper and the grated nutmeg. Transfer the spinach to a large bowl and mix in the ricotta, Parmesan cheese, eggs and flour. Beat the mixture well until it is smooth.

2 Shape the mixture into ovals with two teaspoons and place them on a lightly floured tray. Chill for 30 minutes.

3 Have a large, shallow pan of simmering, salted water ready. Cook the gnocchi in two batches, for about 5 minutes. As soon as the gnocchi rise to the surface, remove them with a slotted spoon and drain on a clean dishcloth.

4 Preheat the oven to 350°F. For the sauce, melt the butter in a pan, add the flour and blend in the milk. Boil until thickened, and season.

5 For the vegetable layer, melt the butter and cook the leeks, carrots and celery. Add the zucchini, season and stir. Transfer to a 10-cup ovenproof dish.

6 Place the drained gnocchi on top of the vegetables, spoon on the sauce and sprinkle with grated cheese. Bake for 30 minutes, or until golden brown.

VEGETABLE GOUGÈRE

This makes a light vegetarian supper or a main course served with baked potatoes.

INGREDIENTS

4 tablespoons (½ stick) butter
⅔ cup water
⅔ cup flour
2 eggs, beaten
¼ teaspoon English mustard powder
2 ounces Gruyère or Cheddar cheese, cubed
salt and freshly ground black pepper
2 teaspoons chopped fresh parsley, to garnish

For the Filling
2 tablespoons butter
1 onion, sliced
1 garlic clove, crushed
3 cups sliced mushrooms
1 tablespoon flour
1 can (14 ounces) tomatoes, plus their juice
1 teaspoon superfine sugar
2 small or 1 large zucchini, thickly sliced

For the Topping
1 tablespoon grated Parmesan cheese
1 tablespoon bread crumbs, toasted

Serves 4

2 Beat the eggs into the paste. Season, add the mustard powder and fold in the cheese. Set aside.

3 For the filling, melt the butter and cook the onion. Add the garlic and mushrooms and cook for 3 minutes. Stir in the flour and tomatoes. Bring to a boil, stirring. Add the sugar; season with salt, pepper. Add the zucchini.

4 Butter a 5-cup ovenproof dish. Spoon the choux pastry in rough mounds around the sides of the dish and transfer the filling to the center. Sprinkle the Parmesan cheese and bread crumbs on top of the filling. Bake for 35–40 minutes, or until the pastry is well risen and golden brown. Sprinkle with chopped parsley and serve hot.

1 Preheat the oven to 400°F. To make the choux pastry, melt the butter in a large pan, add the water and bring to a boil. As soon as the liquid is boiling, draw the pan away from the heat and beat in the flour all at once. Continue beating until a smooth, glossy paste is formed. Transfer the paste to a large mixing bowl and set aside to let cool slightly.

CHEESE, RICE AND VEGETABLE STRUDEL

Based on a traditional Russian dish called "Koulibiac," this makes a perfect vegetarian

main course or, for meat eaters, a welcome accompaniment to cold leftover turkey or sliced ham.

INGREDIENTS

1 cup long-grain rice
2 tablespoons butter
1–2 leeks, thinly sliced
5 cups mushrooms, sliced
8 ounces Gruyère or Cheddar cheese,
grated
8 ounces feta cheese, cubed
2 tablespoons currants
½ cup chopped almonds or hazelnuts,
toasted
2 tablespoons chopped fresh parsley
1 package (10 ounces) frozen filo pastry,
thawed
2 tablespoons olive oil
salt and freshly ground black pepper

Serves 8

1 Cook the rice in boiling, salted water for 10–12 minutes, until tender but still with a little "bite." Drain, rinse under cold running water and set aside to drain again. Melt the butter and cook the leeks and mushrooms for 5 minutes. Transfer to a large bowl and set aside until the vegetables have cooled.

2 Add the well-drained rice, the cheeses, currants, toasted almonds and chopped fresh parsley; season to taste. (You may not need to add very much salt, as the feta cheese is very salty.)

3 Preheat the oven to 375°F. Unwrap the filo pastry. Cover it with a piece of plastic wrap and a clean damp cloth while you work, to prevent it from drying out. Lay a sheet of filo pastry on a large piece of waxed paper and brush it with oil. Lay a second sheet on top, overlapping the first by 1 inch. Put another sheet with its long side running at right angles to the first two. Lay a fourth sheet in the same way, overlapping by 1 inch. Continue in this way, alternating the layers of two sheets so that the seam between the two sheets runs in the opposite direction for each layer.

4 Place the filling mixture along the center of the pastry sheet and carefully shape it with your hands into a rectangle that measures approximately 4 x 12 inches.

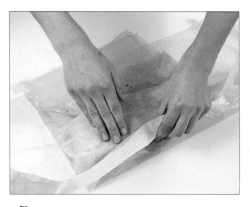

5 Fold the layers of filo pastry over the filling and carefully roll it over, with the help of the waxed paper, so that the seam ends up being hidden on the underside of the strudel.

6 Lift the strudel onto a greased baking sheet and gently tuck the edges under, so that the filling does not escape during cooking. Brush with oil and bake for 30–40 minutes, or until golden brown and crisp. Let the strudel stand for 5 minutes before cutting into thick slices. Serve immediately or freeze until needed.

COOK'S TIP

The traditional Koulibiac dish has slices of hard-cooked egg as an ingredient in the filling—you could add it if desired.

VEGETABLE CRUMBLE WITH ANCHOVIES

The anchovies may be left out of this dish so that vegetarians can enjoy it, but they do give the

vegetables a delicious flavor. Serve the dish on its own or as an accompaniment to sliced turkey or ham.

INGREDIENTS

1 pound potatoes
2 leeks
2 tablespoons butter
1 pound carrots, chopped
2 garlic cloves, crushed
3 cups mushrooms, sliced
1 pound Brussels sprouts, sliced
1 can (2 ounces) anchovies, drained
salt and freshly ground black pepper

For the Cheese Crumble
¼ cup flour
4 tablespoons (½ stick) butter
1 cup fresh bread crumbs
½ cup grated Cheddar cheese
2 tablespoons chopped fresh parsley
1 teaspoon English mustard powder

Serves 8

2 Melt the butter and cook the leeks and carrots for 2–3 minutes. Add the garlic and sliced mushrooms and cook for another 3 minutes. Add the Brussels sprouts. Season with pepper only, if using the anchovies. If not, add salt to taste. Transfer to a 10-cup ovenproof dish.

4 To make the crumble, sift the flour into a bowl and rub in the butter until the mixture resembles fine bread crumbs, or process in a food processor. Add the bread crumbs, fold in the grated cheese and add the chopped fresh parsley and the mustard powder. Combine well. Spoon the crumble over the vegetables and bake for 20–30 minutes, or until the crumble topping is golden and crispy.

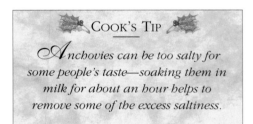

🌿 COOK'S TIP 🌿

Anchovies can be too salty for some people's taste—soaking them in milk for about an hour helps to remove some of the excess saltiness.

1 Peel and halve the potatoes and parboil them in salted water until just tender. Drain and cool. Cut the leeks in half lengthwise and wash them thoroughly to remove any small pieces of grit or soil. Drain on paper towels and slice into ½-inch pieces.

3 Preheat the oven to 400°F. Chop the anchovies and scatter them over the vegetables. Slice the cooked potatoes and arrange them on top of the anchovies.

CHEESE AND SPINACH TART

This tart freezes well and can be reheated. It makes an excellent addition to a festive buffet party.

INGREDIENTS

8 tablespoons (1 stick) butter
2 cups flour
½ teaspoon English mustard powder
½ teaspoon paprika
large pinch of salt
1 cup grated Cheddar cheese
3–4 tablespoons cold water
1 egg, beaten, to glaze

For the Filling
1 pound frozen spinach
1 onion, chopped
pinch of grated nutmeg
1 cup cottage cheese
2 large eggs
2 ounces Parmesan cheese, grated
⅔ cup light cream or half-and-half
salt and freshly ground black pepper

Serves 8

1 Using your fingertips, rub the butter into the flour until it resembles fine bread crumbs. Rub in the next four ingredients. Alternatively, process in a food processor. Bind to a dough with the cold water. Knead until smooth and pliable, wrap in plastic wrap and chill for about 30 minutes.

2 Put the spinach and onion in a pan, cover, and cook slowly. Increase the heat to boil off any water. Season with salt, pepper and nutmeg. Transfer the spinach to a bowl and cool slightly. Add the remaining filling ingredients.

3 Preheat the oven to 400°F. Put a baking sheet in the oven to preheat. Reserve one-third of the pastry for the lid. Roll out the remaining pastry and line a 9-inch loose-bottomed tart pan. Press the pastry into the edges and crimp the top edge. Remove any excess pastry. Pour the filling into the pastry shell.

4 Roll out the remaining pastry and cut it with a lattice pastry cutter. Carefully open the lattice. Using a rolling pin, lay it over the tart. Brush the seams with egg glaze. Press the edges together and trim off any excess. Brush the lattice with egg glaze and bake for 40 minutes, until golden brown. Serve hot or cold.

Chestnut and Mushroom Loaf

You can prepare this dish ahead, freezing it unbaked. Thaw at room temperature overnight before baking.

Ingredients

3 tablespoons olive oil, plus extra for brushing
2 medium onions, chopped
2 cloves garlic, chopped
1¼ cups chopped button mushrooms
½ cup red wine
1 can (8 ounces) unsweetened chestnut purée
1 cup fresh whole-wheat bread crumbs
salt and freshly ground black pepper
¾ cup fresh cranberries, plus extra to decorate
1 pound pastry
flour, for dusting
1 small egg, beaten, to glaze

Serves 8

1 Preheat the oven to 375°F. Heat the oil in a pan and fry the onions over medium heat until they are translucent. This will take 7–8 minutes. Add the chopped garlic and mushrooms and fry for another 3 minutes. Pour in the wine, stir well and simmer over low heat until it has evaporated, stirring occasionally. Remove from the heat, stir in the chestnut purée and bread crumbs and season with salt and pepper. Set aside to cool.

2 Simmer the cranberries in a little water for 5 minutes, until they start to pop, then drain and let cool.

3 Lightly brush a 2½-cup loaf pan with oil. On a lightly floured surface, roll out the pastry to a thickness of about ¼ inch. Cut rectangles to fit the base and sides of the pan and press them in place. Press the edges together to seal them. Cut a piece of pastry to fit the top of the pan and set it aside.

4 Spoon half the chestnut mixture into the pan and level the surface. Sprinkle on a layer of the cranberries and cover with the remaining chestnut mixture. Cover the filling with the pastry lid and pinch the edges to attach them to the sides. Dust the work surface with flour, then cut shapes from the pastry trimmings to use as decorations.

5 Brush the pastry top and the decorative shapes with the beaten egg glaze and arrange the shapes in a pattern on top.

6 Bake the loaf for 35 minutes, or until the top is golden brown. Decorate the top with fresh cranberries. Serve hot.

Spiced Vegetable Couscous

Couscous, a pasta make from semolina, is popular throughout North Africa, mostly in Morocco.

It is traditionally served with Moroccan vegetable stews or tagines but makes a fabulous alternative

Christmas dish. You can serve it on its own or with roasted meat or poultry.

INGREDIENTS

3 tablespoons vegetable oil
1 large onion, finely chopped
2 garlic cloves, crushed
1 tablespoon tomato paste
½ teaspoon ground turmeric
½ teaspoon cayenne pepper
1 teaspoon ground coriander
1 teaspoon ground cumin
½ small cauliflower, broken into florets
8 ounces baby carrots
1 red bell pepper, seeded and diced
4 beefsteak tomatoes
1 zucchini, thickly sliced
1 can (14 ounces) chickpeas, drained and rinsed
3 tablespoons chopped fresh cilantro
salt and freshly ground black pepper
cilantro sprigs, to garnish

For the Couscous
2⅔ cups couscous
1 teaspoon salt
2 tablespoons butter

Serves 6

2 Add the cauliflower, carrots and red pepper, with enough water to come halfway up the vegetables. Bring to a boil, then lower the heat, cover and simmer for 10 minutes.

3 Plunge the tomatoes into boiling water for 30 seconds, then refresh in cold water. Peel off the skins and chop. Add the sliced zucchini, chickpeas and tomatoes to the other vegetables and cook for another 10 minutes. Stir in the chopped cilantro and season with salt and pepper. Set aside and keep hot.

4 To cook the couscous, bring 2 cups water to a boil in a large saucepan. Add the remaining 1 tablespoon oil and the salt. Remove from the heat and add the couscous, stirring. Let swell for 2 minutes, then add the butter and heat through, stirring to separate the grains.

5 Transfer the couscous to a warm serving dish and spoon the vegetables on top, pouring any liquid over them. Garnish with the cilantro sprigs and serve immediately.

❦ COOK'S TIP ❦

*B*eefsteak tomatoes have excellent flavor and are ideal for this recipe, but you can substitute six ordinary tomatoes or two 14-ounce cans chopped tomatoes, if beefsteak tomatoes are not available.

1 Heat 2 tablespoons of the oil in a large pan, add the onion and garlic, and cook until soft and translucent. Stir in the tomato paste, turmeric, cayenne, ground coriander and cumin. Cook, stirring, for 2 minutes.

Filo Vegetable Pie

This stunning pie packed with winter vegetables, fruit, cheese and nuts makes a delicious main course

for vegetarians. For meat eaters, it is an excellent accompaniment to

cold sliced turkey or other meat dishes.

INGREDIENTS

2 leeks
11 tablespoons butter
4 carrots, cubed
3 cups sliced mushrooms
8 ounces Brussels sprouts, quartered
2 garlic cloves, crushed
½ cup cream cheese
½ cup Roquefort or Stilton cheese
⅔ cup heavy cream
2 eggs, beaten
2 apples
1 cup cashews or pine nuts, toasted
1 package (12 ounces) frozen filo pastry, defrosted
salt and freshly ground black pepper

Serves 6–8

3 Whisk the cream cheese and blue cheese, cream, eggs and seasoning together in a bowl. Pour them over the vegetables. Peel and core the apples and cut into ½-inch cubes. Stir them into the vegetables. Lastly, add the toasted cashew or pine nuts.

5 Spoon in the vegetable mixture and fold over the excess filo pastry to cover the filling.

6 Brush the remaining filo sheets with butter and cut them into 1-inch strips. Cover the top of the pie with these strips, arranging them in a rough mound. Bake for 35–45 minutes, or until golden brown all over. Let stand for 5 minutes, and then unclip the spring and gently remove the sides of the cake pan. Transfer the pie to a large plate.

1 Preheat the oven to 350°F. Cut the leeks in half through the root and wash them, separating the layers slightly to check that they are clean. Slice into ½-inch pieces, drain and dry.

2 Heat 3 tablespoons of the butter in a large pan and cook the leeks and carrots, covered, over medium heat for 5 minutes. Add the mushrooms, Brussels sprouts and garlic and cook for another 2 minutes. Transfer the vegetables to a bowl and let them cool.

4 Melt the remaining butter. Brush it all over the inside of a 9-inch springform cake pan. Brush two-thirds of the filo pastry sheets with butter, one sheet at a time, and use them to line the base and sides of the pan, overlapping the layers so that there are no gaps for the filling to fall through.

COOK'S TIP

When working with filo pastry, always keep the sheets you are not using under a clean, damp cloth to prevent them from drying out.

PUMPKIN GNOCCHI

Gnocchi is an Italian pasta dumpling usually made from potatoes; in this special recipe,

pumpkin is added, too. A chanterelle sauce provides both richness and flavor.

INGREDIENTS

1 pound potatoes, peeled
1 large wedge (about 1 pound) pumpkin,
peeled and chopped
2 egg yolks
1¾ cups flour
pinch of ground allspice
¼ teaspoon ground cinnamon
pinch of grated nutmeg
finely grated rind of ½ orange
salt and freshly ground black pepper

For the Sauce
2 tablespoons olive oil
1 shallot
6 ounces chanterelles, sliced, or
¼ cup dried, soaked in warm water
2 teaspoons almond butter
⅔ cup crème fraîche
a little milk or water
5 tablespoons chopped fresh parsley
½ cup grated Parmesan cheese

Serves 4

1 Cover the potatoes with cold salted water, bring to a boil and cook for 20 minutes. Drain and set aside. Wrap the pumpkin in foil and bake at 350°F for 30 minutes. Drain well, then add to the potato and pass through a vegetable mill into a bowl. Add the egg yolks, flour, spices, orange rind and seasoning and mix well to make a soft dough. Add more flour if necessary.

2 Bring a large pan of salted water to a boil, then dredge a work surface with flour. Spoon the gnocchi mixture into a piping bag fitted with a ½-inch plain nozzle. Pipe onto the floured surface to make a 6-inch sausage shape. Roll in flour and cut into 1-inch pieces. Repeat the process, making more sausage shapes, until the dough is used up. Mark each gnocchi lightly with a fork and cook for 3–4 minutes in the boiling water.

3 Meanwhile, make the sauce. Heat the oil in a nonstick frying pan. Add the shallot and fry until soft, without coloring. Add the chanterelles and cook briefly, then add the almond butter. Stir to melt, then stir in the crème fraîche. Simmer briefly and adjust the consistency with milk. Add the parsley and season to taste.

Right: This Spinach and Ricotta Gnocchi makes a quick variation. Cook 2lb spinach in a saucepan and process in a blender or food processor. Mix with 1½ cups ricotta cheese, 4 tbsp freshly grated Parmesan cheese and 3 beaten eggs. Season to taste. Add enough plain flour to make a soft dough and shape into 3in sausages. Cook the gnocchi in salted boiling water for 1–2 minutes. Transfer to a serving dish, pour over ½ cup melted butter and sprinkle with grated Parmesan cheese, to serve.

4 Lift the gnocchi out of the water with a slotted spoon, transfer into warmed bowls and spoon the chanterelle sauce over the top. Scatter the grated Parmesan cheese on top and serve immediately.

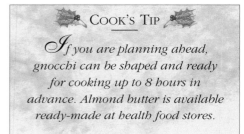

COOK'S TIP

If you are planning ahead, gnocchi can be shaped and ready for cooking up to 8 hours in advance. Almond butter is available ready-made at health food stores.

Festive Brussels Sprouts

Be sure to allow plenty of time to peel the chestnuts; the process is time-consuming but well worth the effort.

INGREDIENTS

1 pound fresh chestnuts
2 cups vegetable stock
1 pound Brussels sprouts
1 pound carrots
2 tablespoons butter
salt and freshly ground black pepper

Serves 8

1 Using a knife, peel the raw chestnuts, leaving the brown, papery skins intact. Bring a small pan of water to a boil, drop a handful of chestnuts at a time into the water for a few minutes, and remove with a slotted spoon.

2 Put the peeled chestnuts in a pan with the stock. Cover and bring to a boil. Simmer for 10 minutes. Drain.

3 Peel and trim the sprouts. Boil in salted water for 5 minutes. Drain.

4 Cut the carrots in ½-inch diagonal slices. Put them in a pan with cold water to cover, bring to a boil and simmer for 6 minutes. Drain. Melt the butter in a clean pan, add the chestnuts, sprouts and carrots and season. Serve hot.

Creamy Spinach Purée

Crème fraîche, the thick French sour cream, or béchamel sauce usually gives this spinach recipe

its creamy richness, but try this quick, light alternative.

INGREDIENTS

1½ pounds spinach, stems removed
1 cup cream cheese
milk (if needed)
freshly grated nutmeg
salt and freshly ground black pepper

Serves 4

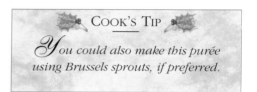

COOK'S TIP

You could also make this purée using Brussels sprouts, if preferred.

1 Rinse the spinach thoroughly, taking care to remove any grit or soil clinging to the leaves. Spin or shake lightly and place in a deep frying pan or wok with just the water clinging to the leaves. Cook, uncovered, over medium heat for 3–4 minutes, until wilted. Drain the spinach in a colander or large sieve, pressing out the excess moisture with the back of a spoon; the spinach doesn't need to be completely dry.

3 Season the spinach mixture with salt, pepper and nutmeg. Transfer to a heavy pan and reheat gently over low heat. Place in a serving dish and serve hot.

2 In a food processor fitted with a metal blade, purée the spinach and cream cheese until well blended, then transfer the mixture to a large bowl. If the purée is too thick to fall easily from a spoon, add a little of the milk, spoonful by spoonful.

Leek and Onion Tart

This unusual recipe isn't a normal tart with pastry, but an all-in-one savory treat

that is excellent served as an accompaniment to roast meat.

Ingredients

4 tablespoons (½ stick) unsalted butter
8 leeks, sliced thinly
2 large onions, sliced thinly
2 cups self-rising flour
½ cup solid vegetable shortening
⅔ cup water
salt and freshly ground black pepper

Serves 4

1 Preheat the oven to 400°F. Melt the butter in a pan and sauté the leeks and onions until soft. Season well with salt and black pepper.

2 Mix the flour, shortening and water together in a large bowl to make a soft but sticky dough. Mix into the leek mixture in the pan. Place the contents of the pan in a greased shallow ovenproof dish and level the surface with a spatula. Bake for about 30 minutes, or until brown and crispy. Serve the tart sliced, as a vegetable side dish.

Cook's Tip

Onions keep very well stored in a cool, dry place. Do not store them in the fridge, as they will go soft, and never keep cut onions in the fridge unless you want onion-scented milk and an onion-scented home.

Thyme-Roasted Onions

These slow-roasted onions develop a delicious, sweet flavor that is the perfect accompaniment

to roast meat. You could prepare parboiled new potatoes in the same way.

Ingredients

5 tablespoons olive oil
4 tablespoons (½ stick) unsalted butter
2 pounds small onions
2 tablespoons chopped fresh thyme
salt and freshly ground black pepper

Serves 4

Cook's Tip

Baby yellow or Vidalia onions would be perfect for this dish, as both types are recommended for slow-roasting. Shallots could be used as a very pleasant alternative; they also taste excellent cooked in this way.

2 Add the thyme and seasoning and roast for 45 minutes, basting regularly.

1 Preheat the oven to 425°F. Heat the oil and butter in a large roasting pan. Remove the outer layer of skin from the onions but keep them whole. Add the onions to the roasting pan and toss them in the oil and butter mixture over a medium heat until they are very lightly sautéed.

81

Sweet-and-Sour Red Cabbage

This cabbage dish can be cooked the day before and reheated for serving. It is a good

accompaniment to goose, pork or strong-flavored game dishes.

Ingredients

2 pounds red cabbage
2 tablespoons olive oil
2 large onions, sliced
2 large apples, peeled, cored and sliced
2 tablespoons cider vinegar
2 tablespoons light brown sugar
8 ounces bacon, chopped (optional)
salt and freshly ground black pepper

Serves 8

1 Preheat the oven to 350°F. Cut the cabbage into quarters and shred it finely with a sharp knife.

2 Heat the oil in a large ovenproof casserole. Cook the onion over low heat for 2 minutes.

3 Stir the cabbage, apples, vinegar, sugar and seasoning into the casserole. Cover and cook for 1 hour, until tender. Stir halfway through cooking.

4 Fry the bacon, if using, until crisp. Stir it into the cabbage before serving.

PARSNIP AND CHESTNUT CROQUETTES

This is a delightful way to present classic Christmas vegetables.

INGREDIENTS

*1 pound parsnips, cut roughly into small
pieces*
4 ounces frozen chestnuts
2 tablespoons butter
1 garlic clove, crushed
1 tablespoon chopped fresh cilantro
1 egg, beaten
½ cup fresh white bread crumbs
vegetable oil, for frying
salt and freshly ground black pepper
sprig of cilantro, to garnish

Makes 10–12

1 Place the parsnips in a saucepan with enough water to cover. Bring to a boil, cover and simmer for 15–20 minutes, until completely tender.

2 Place the frozen chestnuts in a pan of water, bring to a boil and simmer for 8–10 minutes, until very tender. Drain, then place the chestnuts in a mixing bowl and mash roughly.

3 Melt the butter in a small saucepan and cook the garlic for 30 seconds. Drain the parsnips and mash with the garlic butter. Stir in the chestnuts and chopped cilantro, then season well.

4 Take about 1 tablespoon of the mixture at a time and form into 3-inch-long croquettes. Dip into the beaten egg, then roll in bread crumbs.

5 Heat a little oil in a frying pan and fry the croquettes for 3–4 minutes, or until golden, turning frequently so they brown evenly. Drain on paper towels and then serve immediately, garnished with a fresh cilantro sprig.

COOK'S TIP

The addition of the chestnuts gives the dish a festive flavor. If you are unable to find frozen chestnuts, you could use unsweetened peeled chestnuts available in cans at supermarkets.

GLAZED CARROTS WITH CIDER

This dish is extremely simple to make. The carrots are cooked in a minimum of liquid

to bring out their best flavor, and the cider adds a pleasant sharpness.

INGREDIENTS

1 pound young carrots
2 tablespoons butter
1 tablespoon light brown sugar
½ cup cider
¼ cup vegetable stock or water
1 teaspoon Dijon mustard
1 tablespoon finely chopped fresh parsley

Serves 4

1 Trim the tops and bottoms off all of the carrots. Peel or scrape them. Using a sharp knife, cut them into julienne strips.

2 Melt the butter in a heavy frying pan, add the carrots and sauté for 4–5 minutes, stirring frequently. Sprinkle with the sugar and cook, stirring, for 1 minute, or until the sugar has dissolved.

3 Add the cider and stock to the frying pan. Bring to a boil and stir in the Dijon mustard. Partially cover the pan with the lid and simmer for 10–12 minutes, or until the carrots are just tender. Remove the lid and continue cooking until the liquid has reduced to a thick sauce.

4 Remove the pan from the heat and stir in the chopped fresh parsley. Spoon the carrots into a warmed serving dish. Serve as an accompaniment to grilled meat or fish or with a vegetarian dish.

COOK'S TIP

If the carrots are cooked before the liquid in the saucepan has reduced, transfer the carrots to a dish and rapidly boil the liquid until thick. Pour the sauce over the carrots and sprinkle with parsley.

Stir-Fried Brussels Sprouts

Many people are very wary of eating Brussels sprouts because they have had too many

overcooked sprouts served to them in the past. This recipe makes the most of the

vegetable's flavor and has the added interest of an Asian twist.

INGREDIENTS

1 pound Brussels sprouts
1 tablespoon sunflower oil
6–8 scallions, cut into 1-inch lengths
2 slices fresh ginger
⅓ cup slivered almonds
⅔–¾ cup vegetable or chicken stock
salt

Serves 4

1 Remove any large outer leaves and trim the bases of the Brussels sprouts. Cut into slices about ½ inch thick.

2 Heat the oil in a wok or heavy frying pan and fry the scallions and the fresh ginger for 2–3 minutes, stirring frequently. Add the almonds and stir-fry over medium heat until both the scallions and almonds begin to brown.

3 Remove and discard the ginger, reduce the heat and stir in the Brussels sprouts. Stir-fry for a few minutes and then pour in the vegetable stock and cook over low heat for 5–6 minutes or until the sprouts are nearly tender.

4 Add a little salt to the wok or frying pan, if necessary, and then increase the heat to boil off the excess liquid. Spoon the Brussels sprouts into a warmed serving dish and serve immediately.

COOK'S TIP

If you want to further enhance the Asian flavor of this dish, you could add a couple dashes of light soy sauce.

PEAS WITH BABY ONIONS AND CREAM

Ideally, use fresh peas and fresh baby onions for this dish. Frozen peas

can be used if fresh ones aren't available, but frozen onions tend to be insipid

and are not worth using. Alternatively, you could use the white part of scallions.

INGREDIENTS

2–3 cups baby onions
1 tablespoon butter
2 pounds fresh peas or
3 cups fresh or frozen peas
⅔ cup heavy cream
1 tablespoon flour
2 teaspoons chopped fresh parsley
1–2 tablespoons lemon juice (optional)
salt and freshly ground black pepper

Serves 4

1 Remove the outer layer of skin from the onions and then halve them, if necessary. Melt the butter in a flameproof casserole and fry the onions for 5–6 minutes over medium heat, until they are tender and just beginning to brown.

2 Add the peas and stir-fry for a few minutes. Add ½ cup water and bring to a boil. Simmer for about 10 minutes, until both are tender. There should be a thin layer of water on the bottom of the pan.

3 Blend the cream with the flour. Remove the frying pan from the heat, stir in the cream mixture and fresh parsley and season to taste.

4 Cook over low heat for 3–4 minutes, or until the sauce is thick. Add a little lemon juice, if using.

GREEN BEANS WITH BACON AND CREAM

This baked vegetable accompaniment is rich and full of flavor. It would taste particularly

good served alongside any number of chicken dishes.

INGREDIENTS

12 ounces green beans
4 strips bacon, chopped
2 tablespoons (¼ stick) butter
or margarine
1 tablespoon flour
1½ cups half-and-half
salt and freshly ground black pepper

Serves 4

1 Preheat the oven to 375°F. Trim the beans and cook in lightly salted boiling water for about 5 minutes, until just tender. Drain and place them in an ovenproof dish.

2 Fry the bacon until crisp, stirring constantly to make sure that it doesn't stick to the frying pan. Crumble the bacon into very small pieces. Stir into the ovenproof dish with the beans and set aside.

3 Melt the butter in a large saucepan, stir in the flour and then add the half-and-half to make a smooth sauce, stirring continuously. Season well with plenty of salt and freshly ground black pepper.

4 Pour the sauce over the beans and bacon in the dish and carefully mix it in. Cover the dish lightly with a piece of foil and bake for 15–20 minutes or until hot. Serve immediately.

GRATIN DAUPHINOIS

This dish can be made and baked in advance; reheat it in the oven for 20–30 minutes before serving.

This is a good alternative to roast potatoes and needs no last-minute attention.

INGREDIENTS

butter, for greasing
4 pounds potatoes (about 8)
2–3 garlic cloves, crushed
½ teaspoon grated nutmeg
1 cup grated Cheddar cheese
2½ cups milk
1¼ cups light cream or half-and-half
2 large eggs, beaten
salt and freshly ground black pepper

Serves 8

COOK'S TIP

The best type of potatoes to use in this dish are Yukon Gold or baking potatoes. For the cheese, use a full-flavored farmhouse Cheddar for the most satisfying taste.

1 Preheat the oven to 350°F. Butter a 10-cup shallow ovenproof dish. Peel the potatoes, using a potato peeler or a sharp knife, and slice them thinly. If you have a food processor, slice the potatoes in it, using the metal blade.

2 Layer the potato slices in the dish. Add the crushed garlic, nutmeg and two-thirds of the grated Cheddar cheese in alternate layers with the potatoes. Season well with salt and freshly ground black pepper.

3 Whisk the milk, cream and eggs together and pour them over the potatoes, making sure the liquid goes all the way to the bottom of the dish.

4 Scatter the remaining cheese on top and bake for 45–50 minutes, or until the top layer is golden brown and the cheese is bubbling. Test the potatoes with a sharp knife; they should be very tender. Serve immediately.

Sautéed Potatoes

These rosemary-scented, crisp golden potatoes are an extra-special treat at Christmastime.

INGREDIENTS

3 pounds baking potatoes (about 6)
4–6 tablespoons oil, bacon drippings or
clarified butter
2 or 3 fresh rosemary sprigs, leaves
removed and chopped
salt and freshly ground black pepper

Serves 6

1 Peel the potatoes and cut into 1-inch pieces. Place them in a bowl, cover with cold water and let soak for 10–15 minutes. Drain, rinse and drain again, then dry thoroughly in a clean dishcloth.

2 In a large, heavy nonstick frying pan or wok, heat about ¼ cup of the oil, drippings or butter over medium-high heat, until very hot but not smoking.

> ❊ COOK'S TIP ❊
>
> *Soaking the potatoes before cooking removes excess starch, resulting in a crispier coating onto the cooked potatoes.*

3 Add the potatoes to the frying pan and cook for 2 minutes, without stirring, so that they brown on one side.

4 Shake the pan and toss the potatoes to brown on the other side. Continue to stir and shake the pan until the potatoes are evenly browned all over. Season with salt and pepper.

5 Add a little more oil, drippings or butter to the frying pan and continue cooking the potatoes over medium-low to low heat for 20–25 minutes, or until tender when pierced with a knife. Stir and shake the pan frequently. About 5 minutes before the end of cooking, sprinkle the potatoes with the chopped fresh rosemary sprigs.

Hasselback Potatoes

This is an unusual way to cook potatoes. Each potato half is sliced almost to the base and then

roasted with oil and butter. The crispy potatoes are then coated in an orange glaze and

returned to the oven until deep golden brown and crunchy.

INGREDIENTS

4 large potatoes
2 tablespoons butter, melted
3 tablespoons olive oil

For the Glaze
juice of 1 orange
grated rind of ½ orange
1 tablespoon brown sugar
freshly ground black pepper

Serves 4–6

1 Preheat the oven to 375°F. Cut each potato in half lengthwise. If you wish to score the potatoes for decoration, place them flat side down on the chopping board and then cut down as if making very thin slices but leaving the bottom ½ inch intact.

2 Place the potatoes in a large roasting dish. Using a pastry brush, coat the potatoes generously with the melted butter. Pour the olive oil over the bottom of the pan and around the potatoes.

3 Bake the potatoes for 40–50 minutes, just until they begin to turn brown.

4 Meanwhile, place the orange juice, orange rind and sugar in a small saucepan and heat gently, stirring, until the sugar has dissolved. Simmer for 3–4 minutes, until the glaze is fairly thick, and then remove from the heat.

5 When the potatoes begin to brown, brush all over with the orange glaze and return to the oven to roast for another 15 minutes, or until the potatoes are a golden brown. Transfer to a warmed serving plate and serve.

Buffet Dishes

$\mathcal{T}$he Christmas Food doesn't have to end with Christmas Day, but you can serve turkey leftovers for only so long. When the guests come on Boxing Day or perhaps New Year's Eve, a buffet is the perfect solution. Tarts and pies are two of the easiest dishes to serve and you'll have a wonderful choice here with the Wild Mushroom Tart, Mini Leek and Onion Tartlets and Turkey and Cranberry Pie. Serve any of these alongside Fillet of Beef with Ratatouille or Classic Whole Salmon, accompanied by Smoked Trout Pilaf or Garden Vegetable Terrine. Provide a little fruit with the tangy Carrot, Apple and Orange Coleslaw, and a few nuts with the Celery, Avocado and Walnut Salad, and you're sure to receive a second day's worth of compliments.

GAME TERRINE

Any game can be used to make this country terrine—rabbit, pheasant or squab—

so choose the best meat your butcher has to offer.

INGREDIENTS

8 ounces bacon
8 ounces lamb's or pig's liver, ground
1 pound ground pork
1 small onion, finely chopped
2 garlic cloves, crushed
2 teaspoons mixed dried herbs
8 ounces game of your choice
¼ cup port or sherry
1 bay leaf
¼ cup flour
1¼ cups aspic jelly, made per package instructions
salt and freshly ground black pepper

Serves 8

2 Mix the ground meats with the chopped onion, garlic and mixed dried herbs. Season well with plenty of salt and ground black pepper.

5 Preheat the oven to 325°F. Put the flour in a small bowl and mix it to a firm dough with 2–3 tablespoons cold water. Cover the terrine with a lid and seal it with the flour paste. Place the terrine in a roasting pan and pour in enough hot water to come halfway up the sides of the pan. Bake for about 2 hours.

1 Separate the bacon into strips and stretch each strip with the back of a heavy kitchen knife. Use the bacon to line a 4-cup terrine. The terrine should be ovenproof and must have a lid to seal in all the flavors during the long cooking time.

3 Use a heavy kitchen knife to cut the game into thin strips, and put the meat in a large mixing bowl with the port. Season with salt and freshly ground black pepper.

4 Put one-third of the ground meat mixture into the terrine. Press the mixture well into the corners. Cover with half the strips of the game and repeat these layers, ending with a ground meat layer. Level the surface and place the bay leaf on top.

6 Remove the lid and weight the terrine down with a 4-pound weight. Let cool. Remove any fat from the surface and cover with warmed aspic jelly. Let sit overnight before turning out onto a serving plate. Serve the terrine cut into thin slices with a mixed salad and some fruit-based chutney.

94

TURKEY AND CRANBERRY PIE

The cranberries add a tart layer to this turkey pie. Cranberry sauce can be used

if fresh cranberries are not available. The pie freezes well and is an ideal dish to prepare in advance.

INGREDIENTS

1 pound pork sausage meat
1 pound lean ground pork
1 tablespoon ground coriander
1 tablespoon mixed dried herbs
finely grated rind of 2 large oranges
2 teaspoons grated fresh ginger or
½ teaspoon ground ginger
1 pound turkey breasts, thinly sliced
1 cup fresh cranberries
salt and freshly ground black pepper

For the Pastry
4 cups flour
1 teaspoon salt
⅔ cup solid vegetable shortening
⅔ cup mixed milk and water

To Finish
1 egg, beaten
1¼ cups aspic jelly, made per package
instructions

Serves 8

1 Preheat the oven to 350°F. Place a large baking sheet in the oven to preheat. In a large bowl, combine the sausage meat, ground pork, ground coriander, mixed dried herbs, orange rind and ginger with plenty of salt and freshly ground black pepper.

2 To make the pastry, put the flour in a large bowl with the salt. Heat the shortening in a pan with the milk and water until just beginning to boil. Take the pan off the heat and let cool slightly.

3 Using a wooden spoon, quickly stir the liquid into the flour until a very stiff dough is formed. Transfer to a work surface and knead until smooth. Cut off one-third the dough for the lid, wrap it in plastic wrap and keep it in a warm place.

4 Roll out the large piece of dough on a floured surface and line the base and sides of a well-greased 8-inch springform cake pan. Work with the dough while it is still warm, as it will start to crack and break if it is allowed to cool.

5 Put the turkey breasts between two pieces of plastic wrap and flatten with a rolling pin to a thickness of ⅛ inch. Spoon half the pork mixture into the base of the pan, pressing it well into the edges. Cover with half of the turkey slices and then the cranberries, followed by the remaining turkey and finally the rest of the pork mixture.

6 Roll out the rest of the dough and cover the filling, trimming any excess and sealing the edges with beaten egg. Make a steam hole in the lid and decorate with pastry trimmings. Brush with beaten egg. Bake for 2 hours. Cover the pie with foil if it gets too brown. Place the pie on a wire rack to cool. When cool, use a funnel to fill the pie with aspic jelly. Let set overnight before unmolding.

FILLET OF BEEF WITH RATATOUILLE

This succulent rare beef is served cold with a colorful garlicky ratatouille.

INGREDIENTS

fillet of beef (about 2 pounds)
3 tablespoons olive oil
1¼ cups aspic jelly, made per package
instructions

For the Marinade
2 tablespoons sherry
2 tablespoons olive oil
2 tablespoons soy sauce
2 teaspoons grated fresh ginger or
1 teaspoon ground ginger
2 garlic cloves, crushed

For the Ratatouille
¼ cup olive oil
1 onion, sliced
2–3 garlic cloves, crushed
1 large eggplant, cubed
1 small red bell pepper, seeded and sliced
1 small green bell pepper, seeded and sliced
1 small yellow bell pepper, seeded and sliced
1 zucchini, sliced
1 pound tomatoes, skinned and quartered
1 tablespoon chopped mixed fresh herbs
2 tablespoons French dressing
salt and freshly ground black pepper

Serves 8

1 Combine all the marinade ingredients in a shallow dish, put the beef in the dish and turn it over to coat it. Cover the dish with plastic wrap and let sit for 30 minutes, to allow the flavors to penetrate.

2 Preheat the oven to 425°F. Using a large slotted spoon, lift the fillet out of the marinade and pat it dry with paper towels. Heat the oil in a frying pan until smoking hot and then brown the beef all over to seal it. Transfer to a roasting pan and roast for 10–15 minutes, basting occasionally with the marinade. Lift the beef onto a large plate and let it cool.

3 Meanwhile, for the ratatouille, heat the oil in a large casserole and cook the onion and garlic over low heat until tender, without letting the onion become brown. Add the eggplant cubes to the casserole and cook for another 5 minutes, until soft. Add the sliced peppers and zucchini and cook for 2 minutes more. Then add the tomatoes, and chopped herbs and season well with salt and pepper. Cook for a few minutes longer.

4 Transfer the ratatouille to a dish and set aside to cool. Drizzle the ratatouille with a little French dressing. Slice the beef and arrange overlapping slices on a serving platter. Brush the slices with cold aspic jelly that is on the point of setting.

5 Let the jelly set completely, then brush with a second coat. Spoon the ratatouille around the beef slices on the platter and serve immediately.

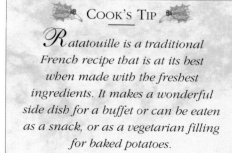

❧ COOK'S TIP ❧

Ratatouille is a traditional French recipe that is at its best when made with the freshest ingredients. It makes a wonderful side dish for a buffet or can be eaten as a snack, or as a vegetarian filling for baked potatoes.

Wild Mushroom Tart

The flavor of wild mushrooms makes this tart really rich. Use as wide a variety of

mushrooms as you can get hold of, for added flavor.

INGREDIENTS

For the Pastry
2 cups flour
½ teaspoon salt
¼ cup solid vegetable shortening
2 teaspoons lemon juice
about ⅔ cup ice water
8 tablespoons (1 stick) butter, cubed
1 egg, beaten

For the Filling
10 tablespoons (1¼ sticks) butter
2 shallots, finely chopped
2 garlic cloves, crushed
1 pound mixed wild mushrooms, sliced
3 tablespoons chopped fresh parsley
2 tablespoons heavy cream
salt and freshly ground black pepper

Serves 6

1 To make the pastry, sift the flour and salt together into a large mixing bowl. Add the vegetable shortening and rub into the mixture until it resembles fine bread crumbs.

2 Add the lemon juice and enough ice water to make a soft but not too sticky dough. Cover and set aside to chill for 20 minutes.

3 Roll the pastry out into a rectangle on a lightly floured surface. Mark the dough into three equal strips and arrange half the butter cubes over two-thirds of the dough.

4 Fold the outer two-thirds over, folding over the uncovered third last. Seal the edges with a rolling pin. Give the dough a quarter turn and roll it out again. Mark it into thirds and dot with the remaining butter in the same way.

5 Chill the pastry for 20 minutes. Repeat the process of marking into thirds, folding over, giving a quarter turn and rolling out three times, chilling for 20 minutes in between each time. To make the filling, melt 4 tablespoons butter and fry the shallots and garlic until soft, but not browned. Add the remaining butter and the mushrooms and cook for 35–40 minutes. Drain off any excess liquid and stir in the remaining ingredients. Let cool. Preheat the oven to 425°F.

6 Divide the pastry in half. Roll out one half into a 9-inch round, cutting around a plate to make a neat shape. Pile the filling into the center. Roll out the remaining pastry large enough to cover the base. Brush the edges of the base with water and then lay the second pastry circle on top. Press the edges together to seal and brush the top with a little beaten egg to glaze. Bake for 45 minutes, or until the pastry has risen and is golden and flaky.

Garden Vegetable Terrine

Perfect for a Christmas buffet menu, this is a softly set, creamy terrine of colorful vegetables

wrapped in glossy spinach leaves. Select large spinach leaves for the best results.

INGREDIENTS

8 ounces fresh leaf spinach
3 carrots, cut into sticks
3–4 long, thin leeks
about 4 ounces green beans, trimmed
1 red bell pepper, cut into strips
2 zucchini, cut into sticks
½ head broccoli, divided into florets

For the Sauce
1 egg and 2 yolks
1¼ cups light cream or half-and-half
fresh nutmeg, grated
1 teaspoon salt
½ cup grated Cheddar cheese
oil, for greasing
freshly ground black pepper

Serves 6

1 Preheat oven to 350°F. Blanch the spinach quickly in boiling water, then drain, refresh in cold water and carefully pat dry.

2 Grease a 6–cup loaf pan and line the base with a sheet of waxed paper. Line with the spinach leaves, letting them overhang the pan.

3 Blanch the rest of the vegetables in boiling, salted water until just tender. Drain and refresh in cold water, then, when cool, pat dry with paper towels.

4 Place the vegetables in the loaf pan in a colorful mixture, making sure the sticks of vegetables lie lengthwise.

5 Beat the sauce ingredients together and slowly pour over the vegetables. Tap the loaf pan to ensure that the sauce seeps into the gaps. Fold over the spinach leaves at the top of the terrine to make a neat surface.

6 Cover the terrine with a sheet of greased foil, then bake in a roasting pan half full of boiling water for 1–1¼ hours, or until set.

7 Cool the terrine in the pan, then chill. To serve, loosen the sides and shake out gently. Serve cut into thick slices.

CHICKEN ROLL

This roll can be prepared and cooked the day before it is needed and will freeze well, too.

Remove from the refrigerator about an hour before serving.

INGREDIENTS

1 chicken (about 4 pounds)

For the Stuffing
1 medium onion, finely chopped
4 tablespoons (½ stick) melted butter
12 ounces lean ground pork
4 strips bacon, chopped
1 tablespoon chopped fresh parsley
2 teaspoons chopped fresh thyme
2 cups fresh white bread crumbs
2 tablespoons sherry
1 large egg, beaten
¼ cup shelled pistachios
¼ cup pitted black olives
(about 12)
salt and freshly ground black pepper

Serves 8

3 Cut the meat off of the carcass, scraping the bones clean. Carefully cut through the sinew around the leg and wing joints and scrape down the bones to free them. Remove the carcass, taking care not to cut through the skin along the breastbone, so that the stuffing will not escape during cooking.

4 To stuff the chicken, lay it flat, skin side down, and level the flesh as much as possible. Shape the stuffing down the center and fold the sides over.

5 Sew the flesh together, using dark thread. (This will be easier to see when the roll is cooked.) Tie with string to form a roll.

6 Preheat the oven to 350°F. Place the roll, with the seam side down, on a roasting rack in a roasting pan and brush with the remaining butter. Bake uncovered for about 1¼ hours, or until cooked. Baste the chicken often. Let cool completely before removing the string and thread. Wrap in foil and chill until ready for serving or freezing.

1 To make the stuffing, cook the chopped onion gently in a frying pan with 2 tablespoons butter until soft. Transfer to a bowl and let cool. Add the remaining ingredients, mix thoroughly and season well with salt and freshly ground black pepper.

2 Set the chicken on a clean cutting board and bone it. To start, use a small, sharp knife to remove the wing tips. Turn the chicken over onto its breast and cut a deep line down the backbone.

MINI LEEK AND ONION TARTLETS

The savory filling in these tartlets is traditional in France, where many types of quiche are popular.

Baking in individual tins makes for easier serving and looks attractive on the buffet table.

INGREDIENTS

2 tablespoons butter
1 onion, thinly sliced
½ teaspoon dried thyme
1 pound leeks, thinly sliced
5 tablespoons grated Gruyère or
Emmenthal cheese
3 eggs
1¼ cups light cream or half-and-half
pinch of freshly grated nutmeg
salt and freshly ground black pepper
lettuce leaves, parsley leaves and cherry
tomatoes, to serve

For the Pastry
1⅓ cups flour
6 tablespoons (¾ stick) cold butter
1 egg yolk
2–3 tablespoons cold water
½ teaspoon salt

Serves 6

1 To make the pastry, sift the flour into a bowl and add the butter. Using your fingertips or a pastry blender, rub or cut the butter into the flour until the mixture resembles fine bread crumbs.

2 Make a well in the flour mixture. In a small bowl, beat together the egg yolk, water and salt. Pour into the well and, using a fork, lightly combine the flour and liquid until the dough begins to stick together. Form into a flattened ball. Wrap and chill for 30 minutes.

3 Lightly butter six 4-inch tartlet pans. On a lightly floured surface, roll out the dough until about ⅛ inch thick. Using a 5-inch fluted cutter, cut out as many rounds as possible. Gently ease the pastry rounds firmly into the bottom and sides of each pan. Reroll the trimmings and use to line the remaining pans. Prick the bottoms all over with a fork and chill for about 30 minutes.

4 Preheat the oven to 375°F. Line the pastry shells with foil and fill each one with baking beans or a heaping handful of dried pulses. Place them on a baking sheet and bake for 6–8 minutes, or until the pastry edges are golden. Lift out the foil and beans and bake the pastry shells for another 2 minutes, until the bottoms appear dry. Transfer to a wire rack and let cool. Reduce the oven temperature to 350°F.

5 In a large frying pan, melt the butter over medium heat, then add the onion and thyme and cook for 3–5 minutes, or until the onion is just softened, stirring frequently. Add the leeks and cook for 10–12 more minutes, or until they are soft and tender. Divide the mixture among the cooled pastry shells and sprinkle the top of each tartlet with cheese, dividing it evenly among them.

6 In a medium-size bowl, beat together the eggs, cream, nutmeg and salt and pepper. Place the pastry shells on a baking sheet and slowly pour in the egg mixture, being careful not to let them overflow. Bake for 15–20 minutes, or until set and golden. Transfer the tartlets to a wire rack to cool slightly, then remove them from the tins and serve warm or at room temperature, with a mixture of lettuce and parsley leaves and cherry tomatoes.

Classic Whole Salmon

Serving a boneless whole salmon is a delight. If you own a fish poacher the method is slightly different:

cover the salmon with water and a dash of white wine, add a bay leaf, sliced lemon and black

peppercorns, and bring to a boil for 6 minutes. Let cool completely in the water.

Drain, pat dry, and continue as instructed in the recipe.

INGREDIENTS

1 whole salmon, about 6 pounds
3 bay leaves
1 lemon, sliced
12 black peppercorns
1¼ cups water
⅔ cup white wine
2 cucumbers, thinly sliced
large bunches of mixed fresh herbs such
as parsley, chervil and chives, to
garnish
mayonnaise, to serve

Serves 8

1 Preheat the oven to 350°F. Clean the inside of the salmon. Rinse the cavity in several changes of cold water and then wipe out with paper towels. Cut the tail into a neat "V" shape with a sharp pair of kitchen scissors. Place the fish on a large piece of double-thick foil. Lay the bay leaves, sliced lemon and black peppercorns inside the cavity. Wrap the foil around the fish and up the sides, and pour in the water and wine. Seal the package tightly and place in a large roasting pan.

2 Bake, allowing 15 minutes per pound plus 15 minutes extra. Remove from the oven and, being careful not to scald yourself on the steam, open up the package. Let cool. Don't be tempted to let the salmon chill overnight, as the skin will be impossible to remove the next day.

3 Using a sharp knife or a sharp pair of kitchen scissors, cut off the head and tail, reserving them if you want to display the whole fish later. Turn the fish upside down on a board so that the flattest side is on top. Carefully peel off the foil and the skin. Using a sharp knife, gently scrape away any excess brown flesh from the pink salmon flesh.

4 Make an incision down the back fillet, drawing the flesh away from the central bone. Take one fillet and place on the serving dish. Remove the second fillet and place it beside the first to form the base of the fish.

5 Carefully remove the backbone from the salmon. Place the other half of the fish, with the skin still intact, flesh side down on top of the base of the fish. Peel off the upper skin and any brown bits. Replace the head and tail if desired. Lay the cucumber slices on top of the fish, working from the tail end until all the flesh is covered and the cucumber resembles scales. Garnish the serving plate with the fresh herbs of your choice. Serve with mayonnaise.

LAYERED SALMON TERRINE

This elegant fish mousse is perfect for a Christmas buffet table or as an appetizer course.

INGREDIENTS

*1 cup milk
4 tablespoons (½ stick) butter
⅔ cup flour
1 pound fresh haddock fillet, boned and
skinned
1 pound fresh salmon fillet, boned and
skinned
2 eggs, beaten
¼ cup heavy cream
4 ounces smoked salmon or trout, cut into
strips
salt and freshly ground black pepper*

Serves 8

1 Heat the milk and butter in a saucepan until the milk is boiling. Take the saucepan off of the heat and beat in the flour until a thick, smooth paste forms. Season well with salt and freshly ground black pepper, and transfer the flour paste to a plate and let cool.

2 Put the haddock in a food processor and process it until smooth. Put it in a bowl. Process the salmon fillet in the same way and put it in a separate bowl. Add an egg and half the cream to each of the fish mixtures. Then beat in half the milk and flour paste into each mixture.

3 Preheat the oven to 350°F. Butter a 6–cup loaf pan and line it with a piece of waxed paper. Lay strips of smoked salmon diagonally over the bottom and up the side of the lined pan.

4 Spoon the haddock mixture into the pan and level the surface. Cover with the salmon mixture and level the surface.

5 Cover the pan with a layer of buttered waxed paper and a layer of foil. Place it in a roasting pan and half fill the pan with hot water. Cook for 40 minutes.

6 Remove the terrine from the oven and let stand for 10 minutes. Remove the terrine from the loaf pan and serve it warm or let it cool, as preferred.

Smoked Trout Pilaf

Smoked trout might seem an unusual partner for rice, but this is a winning combination with an original,

Indian-influenced flavor that will be greatly appreciated at Christmastime.

INGREDIENTS

1¼ cups white basmati rice
3 tablespoons butter
2 onions, sliced into rings
1 garlic clove, crushed
2 bay leaves
2 whole cloves
2 green cardamom pods
2 cinnamon sticks
1 teaspoon cumin seeds
4 smoked trout fillets, (8 ounces each)
½ cup slivered almonds, toasted
⅓ cup raisins
2 tablespoons chopped fresh parsley
mango chutney and poppadums, to serve

Serves 4

COOK'S TIP

The recommendation of mango chutney and poppadums as a serving suggestion with this dish really shows that alternative fare at Christmas can be extremely festive. Ready-made poppadums can easily be found at specialty stores and supermarkets. They can be heated in the oven or a microwave in just a few minutes.

1 Wash the rice thoroughly in several changes of water and drain well. Set aside. Melt the butter in a large frying pan and fry the onions until well browned, stirring frequently.

2 Add the garlic, bay leaves, cloves, cardamom pods, cinnamon sticks and cumin seeds and stir-fry for 1 minute.

3 Stir in the rice, then add 2½ cups boiling water. Bring to a boil. Cover the pan tightly, reduce the heat and cook very gently for 20–25 minutes, or until the water has been absorbed and the rice is tender.

4 Flake the smoked trout and add to the pan with the almonds and raisins. Fork through gently. Re-cover the pan and let the smoked trout warm in the rice for a few minutes. Remove the spices and bay leaves. Scatter the parsley on top and serve with mango chutney and poppadums.

Tomato and Basil Tart

This mouthwatering savory tart will be very popular at buffet parties, and vegetarians will love it too.

It is very simple to make, with rich unsweetened pastry topped with slices of mozzarella cheese

and tomatoes and enriched with olive oil and basil leaves.

INGREDIENTS

5 ounces mozzarella, thinly sliced
4 large tomatoes, thickly sliced
about 10 basil leaves
2 tablespoons olive oil
2 garlic cloves, thinly sliced
sea salt and freshly ground black pepper

For the Pastry
1 cup flour
pinch of salt
4 tablespoons (½ stick) butter or margarine
1 egg yolk

Serves 4

1 To prepare the pastry, combine the flour and salt, then rub in the butter and egg yolk. Add enough cold water to make a smooth dough and knead lightly on a floured surface. Place in a plastic bag and chill for about 1 hour.

2 Preheat the oven to 375°F. Remove the pastry from the fridge and allow about 10 minutes for it to return to room temperature, then roll out on a lightly-floured surface into an 8-inch round. Press into the bottom of an 8-inch tart or cake pan. Prick the shell all over with a fork and then bake in the preheated oven for about 10 minutes, until the pastry is firm but not brown. Let cool slightly. Reduce the oven temperature to 350°F.

3 Arrange the mozzarella slices over the pastry. On top, arrange a single layer of the sliced tomatoes, overlapping them slightly. Dip the basil leaves in olive oil and arrange them on the tomatoes.

4 Scatter the garlic on top, drizzle with the remaining olive oil and season with a little salt and a good sprinkling of black pepper. Bake for 40–45 minutes, or until the tomatoes are well cooked. Serve hot or at room temperature.

COOK'S TIP

Pricking the base or sides of the pastry before it goes into the oven ensures that the tart does not puff up during the cooking time, making it easier to fill. If the cheese exudes a lot of liquid during baking, tilt the pan and spoon it off to keep the pastry from becoming soggy.

Turkey Rice Salad

A delicious, crunchy salad to use up leftover turkey during the holiday festivities.

INGREDIENTS

1¼ cups brown rice
⅔ cup wild rice
2 red apples, quartered, cored and chopped
2 celery stalks, coarsely sliced
½ bunch seedless grapes
3 tablespoons lemon or orange juice
⅔ cup thick mayonnaise
12 ounces cooked turkey, chopped
salt and freshly ground black pepper
frilly lettuce leaves, to serve

Serves 8

1 Cook the brown and wild rice in boiling salted water for 25 minutes, or until tender. Rinse under cold running water and drain.

2 Transfer the well-drained rice to a large bowl and add the apples, celery and grapes. Beat the lemon juice into the mayonnaise, season with salt and pepper and pour over the rice.

3 Add the turkey and mix well to coat with the lemon mayonnaise.

4 Arrange the frilly lettuce leaves over the bottom and around the sides of a warmed serving dish and spoon the rice on top.

HAM AND BULGUR SALAD

This flavorful, nutty salad is ideal for using up leftover cooked ham for a quick and

simple addition to a Christmas buffet menu.

INGREDIENTS

1⅓ cup bulgur
3 tablespoons olive oil
2 tablespoons lemon juice
1 red bell pepper
1 large slice (8 ounces) cooked ham, diced
2 tablespoons chopped fresh mint
2 tablespoons currants
salt and freshly ground black pepper
sprigs of fresh mint and lemon slices, to
garnish

Serves 8

3 Quarter the bell pepper, removing the stalk and seeds. Rinse under running water. Using a sharp knife, cut the pepper quarters into wide strips and then into diamonds.

4 Add the pepper, ham, chopped fresh mint and currants to the wheat in the bowl. Mix with a spoon to ensure that the ingredients are well distributed, then transfer the salad to a serving dish, garnish with the fresh mint sprigs and lemon slices and serve.

> ### COOK'S TIP
>
> *T*his salad can also be made with 1⅓ cups couscous instead of the bulgur. To prepare, cover the couscous with boiling water as in Step 1.

1 Put the bulgur in a bowl, pour on enough boiling water to cover and let sit until all the water has been absorbed and the grains look as if they have swelled up.

2 Add the oil, lemon juice, and seasoning to taste. Toss to separate the grains, using two forks.

CELERY, AVOCADO AND WALNUT SALAD

The crunchiness of the celery and walnuts contrasts perfectly with the smooth avocado.

Serve it with a sour cream dressing as suggested, or simply dressed with a little

extra-virgin olive oil and freshly squeezed lemon juice.

INGREDIENTS

3 bacon strips (optional)
8 tender celery stalks, very thinly sliced
3 scallions, finely chopped
½ cup chopped walnuts
1 ripe avocado
lemon juice

For the Dressing
½ cup sour cream
1 tablespoon extra-virgin olive oil
pinch of cayenne pepper

Serves 4

1 Fry the bacon, if using, until golden, then chop into small pieces and place in a salad bowl with the celery, scallions and walnuts.

2 Halve the avocado and, using a very sharp knife, cut into thin slices. Peel away the skin from each slice, sprinkle generously with lemon juice and add to the celery mixture.

3 Lightly beat the sour cream, olive oil and cayenne pepper together in a small bowl. Either fold carefully into the salad or serve separately.

COOK'S TIP

Whenever you need to prepare avocado for a salad dish, sprinkle it liberally with lemon juice to prevent the flesh from discoloring before the dish is served.

CARROT, APPLE AND ORANGE COLESLAW

This dish is as delicious as it is easy to make. The garlic and herb dressing adds the

necessary contrast to the sweetness of the salad.

INGREDIENTS

6 carrots, finely grated
2 apples
1 tablespoon lemon juice
1 large orange

For the Dressing
3 tablespoons olive oil
¼ cup sunflower oil
3 tablespoons lemon juice
1 garlic clove, crushed
¼ cup plain yogurt
1 tablespoon chopped mixed fresh herbs
such as tarragon, parsley and chives
salt and freshly ground black pepper

Serves 4

2 Using a sharp knife, remove the peel and pith from the orange and separate it into segments. Add to the carrots and apples.

3 To make the dressing, place both the oils with the lemon juice, crushed garlic, plain yogurt, mixed fresh herbs and seasoning in a jar with a lid and shake to blend.

4 Just before serving, pour the dressing over the salad and toss well to mix.

> ### COOK'S TIP
> *You can prepare the dressing in advance and keep it in the fridge for up to a week.*

1 Place the carrots in a large serving bowl. Quarter the apples, remove the cores and then slice thinly. Sprinkle them with the lemon juice, to prevent them from discoloring, then add to the carrots.

Party Foods

𝒢one are the days of an uninspiring bowl of peanuts or a mediocre offering of cheeses and canapés. The tremendous range of ingredients available in the stores nowadays means that there are endless possibilities for lavish festive party foods. Try mixing a few of these fabulous dishes for a truly international taste: Tapas of Almonds, Olives and Cheese, Shrimp Toasts and Hot Pastrami on a Stick would go together well. For vegetarians, try Mini Filled Baked Potatoes and Spicy Sun-dried Tomato Pizza Wedges. Spoil your guests with mincemeat-filled Filo Crackers, or provide a Rich Chocolate and Fruit Fondue and see them welcome in the New Year around the cooking pot.

CHEESELETS

These crispy cheese crackers are irresistible, and will disappear in moments.

INGREDIENTS

1 cup flour
½ teaspoon salt
½ teaspoon cayenne pepper
½ teaspoon dry mustard
½ cup butter
½ cup grated Cheddar cheese
½ cup grated Gruyère cheese
1 egg white, beaten
1 tablespoon sesame seeds

Makes about 80

1 Preheat the oven to 425°F. Line several baking sheets with parchment paper. Sift the flour, salt, cayenne pepper and mustard into a mixing bowl. Cut the butter into pieces and rub into the flour mixture.

2 Divide the mixture in half, and add the Cheddar to one half and the Gruyère to the other. Using a fork or your fingertips, work each mixture into a soft dough and knead on a floured surface until smooth.

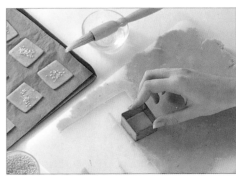

3 Roll out both pieces of dough very thinly and cut into 1-inch squares. Transfer to the lined baking sheets. Brush the squares with beaten egg white, sprinkle with sesame seeds and bake for 5–6 minutes, or until slightly puffed up and pale gold in color. Cool on the baking sheets, then carefully remove with a spatula. Repeat the process until you have used up all the dough. Pack the crackers in airtight tins or present as a gift, packed in boxes tied with ribbon.

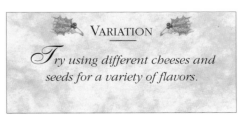

VARIATION

Try using different cheeses and seeds for a variety of flavors.

COCKTAIL CRACKERS

Tiny savory crackers are always a welcome treat.

Experiment with different flavors and shapes, and make a batch of crackers to give as gifts.

INGREDIENTS

3 cups flour
½ teaspoon salt
½ teaspoon black pepper
1 teaspoon whole-grain mustard
6 tablespoons (¾ stick) butter
½ cup grated Cheddar cheese
1 egg, beaten

Flavorings
1 teaspoon chopped nuts
2 teaspoons curry paste
2 teaspoons chili sauce

Makes about 80

2 Knead chopped nuts into one piece, dill seeds into another piece and curry paste and chili sauce into each of the remaining pieces. Wrap each piece of flavored dough in plastic wrap and let chill in the fridge for at least an hour. Remove from the plastic wrap and roll out one piece at a time.

3 Using different-shaped cutters, stamp out about 20 shapes from each piece. Arrange the shapes on the baking sheets and bake for 6–8 minutes, or until slightly puffed up and pale gold in color. Cool on wire racks, then remove the crackers from the baking sheets using a spatula.

1 Preheat the oven to 400°F. Line several baking sheets with parchment paper. Sift the flour into a mixing bowl and add the salt, pepper and mustard. Cut the butter into pieces and rub into the flour mixture until it resembles fine bread crumbs. Use a fork to stir in the cheese and egg, and combine to form a soft dough. Knead lightly on a floured surface and cut into 4 equal pieces.

TAPAS OF ALMONDS, OLIVES AND CHEESE

These three simple ingredients are lightly flavored to create a delicious Spanish tapas medley

that is perfect for a casual appetizer or nibbles to serve with predinner drinks.

INGREDIENTS

½ teaspoon coriander seeds
½ teaspoon fennel seeds
1 teaspoon chopped fresh rosemary
2 teaspoons chopped fresh parsley
2 garlic cloves, crushed
1 tablespoon sherry vinegar
2 tablespoons olive oil
⅔ cup black olives
⅔ cup green olives

For the Marinated Cheese
5 ounces goat cheese
6 tablespoons olive oil
1 tablespoon white wine vinegar
1 teaspoon black peppercorns
1 garlic clove, sliced
3 fresh tarragon or thyme sprigs
tarragon sprigs, to garnish

For the Salted Almonds
¼ teaspoon cayenne pepper
2 tablespoons sea salt
2 tablespoons butter
¼ cup olive oil
1¾ cups blanched almonds
extra sea salt for sprinkling (optional)

Serves 6–8

COOK'S TIP

If serving with predinner drinks, provide toothpicks for spearing the olives and cheese.

1 To make the marinated olives, crush the coriander and fennel seeds with a mortar and pestle. Or, put them into a sturdy plastic bag and crush them with a rolling pin. Combine with the rosemary, parsley, garlic, vinegar and oil and pour over the olives in a small bowl. Cover with plastic wrap and chill for up to 1 week.

2 To make the marinated cheese, cut the cheese into bite-size pieces, leaving the rind on. Combine the oil, vinegar, peppercorns, garlic and herb sprigs and pour over the cheese in a small bowl. Cover with plastic wrap and chill for up to 3 days.

3 To make the salted almonds, combine the cayenne pepper and salt in a large mixing bowl. Melt the butter with the olive oil in a frying pan. Add the almonds to the frying pan and stir-fry for about 5 minutes, or until the almonds are golden.

4 Take the almonds out of the frying pan, pour them into the salt mixture, and toss until the almonds are coated. Let cool, then remove with a slotted spoon and store them in a jar or airtight container for up to 1 week.

5 To serve the tapas, arrange in small, shallow serving dishes. Use fresh sprigs of tarragon to garnish the cheese and scatter a little more salt over the almonds, if desired.

GUACAMOLE

This fiery version of a popular Mexican dish always proves a favorite at parties. The dip can be

served with any number of accompaniments, including tortilla chips, crudités or breadsticks.

INGREDIENTS

2 ripe avocados, peeled and pitted
2 tomatoes, peeled, seeded and finely
chopped
6 scallions, finely chopped
1 or 2 green chilies, seeded and chopped
2 tablespoons fresh lime or lemon juice
1 tablespoon chopped fresh cilantro
salt and freshly ground black pepper
cilantro sprigs, to garnish

Serves 4

1 Put the avocado halves in a large
mixing bowl and mash them roughly
with a large fork.

2 Add the remaining ingredients.
Mix well and season according to taste.
Serve garnished with fresh cilantro.

COOK'S TIP

*When preparing chilies, always be
sure to wash your hands
immediately after slicing them.
The oils released can burn if
you accidentally touch your face
or eyes. If you have sensitive skin,
it is a good idea to wear
a pair of plastic gloves.*

Shrimp Toasts

These crunchy sesame-topped toasts are simple to prepare using a food processor for the shrimp paste.

INGREDIENTS

2 cups cooked, shelled shrimp, well
drained and dried
1 egg white
2 scallions, chopped
1 teaspoon chopped fresh ginger
1 garlic clove, chopped
1 teaspoon cornstarch
½ teaspoon salt
½ teaspoon sugar
2–3 dashes hot pepper sauce
8 slices firm-textured white bread
4–5 tablespoons sesame seeds
vegetable oil, for frying
scallion, to garnish

Makes 64

2 Spread the shrimp paste evenly over the bread slices, then sprinkle on the sesame seeds, pressing to make them stick. Remove the crusts. Cut each slice diagonally into 4 triangles, then cut each in half again to make 64.

3 Heat 2 inches vegetable oil in a heavy saucepan or wok, until hot but not smoking. Fry the triangles for 30–60 seconds, turning once. Drain well and serve hot, garnished with the scallion.

COOK'S TIP

You can prepare these toasts in advance and heat them up in a hot oven before serving. Make sure they are crisp and properly heated, through—they won't be nearly as enjoyable if there's no crunch.

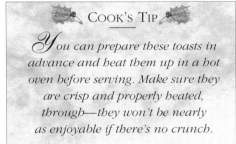

1 For the shrimp paste, put the first 9 ingredients in the bowl of a food processor and process until the mixture forms a smooth paste, scraping down the sides of the bowl occasionally.

PASTRY-WRAPPED CHORIZO PUFFS

These flaky pastry puffs, filled with spicy chorizo sausage and grated cheese, make a perfect

accompaniment to a glass of sherry or cold beer at an informal Christmas party.

INGREDIENTS

8 ounces puff pastry, thawed if frozen
4 ounces cured chorizo sausage,
   chopped
½ cup grated hard cheese
1 small egg, beaten
1 teaspoon paprika

Serves 8

🌿 COOK'S TIP 🌿

*To prepare the chorizo puffs
ahead, chill them without the glaze,
wrapped in a plastic bag, until
ready to bake, then let them
come back to room temperature
while you preheat the oven.
Glaze before baking.*

1 Roll out the pastry thinly on a floured surface. Using a 3-inch cutter, stamp out as many rounds as possible, then reroll the trimmings and stamp out more rounds to make 16 in all.

2 Preheat the oven to 425°F. Toss the chopped chorizo sausage and grated cheese together.

3 Lay one of the pastry rounds on the palm of your hand and place a little of the chorizo mixture across the center.

4 Using your other hand, pinch the edges of the pastry together along the top to seal, as when making a dumpling. Repeat the process with the remaining rounds; you should be able to make 16 puffs in all.

5 Place the pastries on a nonstick baking sheet and brush lightly with the beaten egg to glaze. Using a small sieve or tea strainer, dust the tops lightly with a little of the paprika.

6 Bake the pastries for 10–12 minutes, or until they are puffed and golden brown. Transfer the pastries to a wire rack and let them cool for 5 minutes, then serve them warm, dusted with the rest of the paprika.

Hot Pastrami on a Stick

Because this treat is so quick to make, it is an excellent choice for a party.

INGREDIENTS

vegetable oil, for frying
unsliced rye bread with caraway seeds,
cut into 24 x ½-inch cubes
8 ounces pastrami, in one piece
mild mustard, for spreading
2 pickled cucumbers, cut into small pieces
24 cocktail onions

Makes 24

2 Cut the pastrami into ½-inch cubes on a cutting board, and spread one side of each cube with a little of the mustard.

3 Thread a bread cube onto a toothpick, then a piece of meat with the mustard side against the bread, then a piece of pickled cucumber, and finally an onion. Arrange the toothpicks on a plate or tray, and serve immediately.

COOK'S TIP

For a more traditionally English version of the same dish, use cubes of thick white bread threaded on toothpicks with smoked ham and pickled onions, and served with horseradish sauce.

1 In a heavy, medium frying pan, heat ½ inch of oil. When very hot, but not smoking, add half the bread cubes and fry for about 1 minute, until just golden, turning occasionally. Remove the cubes with a slotted spoon and drain them on paper towels. Repeat with the remaining cubes.

Lamb Tikka

Creamy yogurt and nuts go wonderfully with the spices in these little Indian meatballs.

INGREDIENTS

*1 piece boneless leg of lamb (about
1 pound)
2 scallions, chopped*

*For the Marinade
1½ cups plain yogurt
1 tablespoon ground almonds, cashews or
peanuts
1 tablespoon vegetable oil
2 or 3 garlic cloves, finely chopped
juice of 1 lemon
1 teaspoon garam masala or curry powder
½ teaspoon ground cardamom
¼ teaspoon cayenne pepper
1–2 tablespoons chopped fresh mint*

Makes about 20

1 Prepare the marinade. In a medium bowl, stir together all the ingredients. In a separate small bowl, reserve about ½ cup of the mixture to use as a dipping sauce.

2 Cut the lamb into small pieces and put in a food processor with the scallions. Process until the meat is finely chopped. Add 2–3 tablespoons of the marinade and process again.

3 Test to see if the mixture holds together by pinching a little between your fingertips. Add a little more marinade if necessary, but do not make the mixture too wet and soft.

4 With moistened palms, form the meat mixture into slightly oval-shaped balls about 1½ inches long and arrange in a shallow baking dish. Spoon on the remaining marinade and refrigerate the meatballs for 8–10 hours or overnight.

5 Preheat the broiler and line a baking sheet with foil. Thread each meatball onto a skewer and arrange on the baking sheet. Grill for 4–5 minutes, turning occasionally, until crisp and golden on all sides. Serve with the reserved marinade/dipping sauce.

Chicken Satay with Peanut Sauce

These skewers of marinated chicken can be prepared in advance and served at room temperature.

Beef, pork or even lamb can be used instead of chicken, if you prefer.

INGREDIENTS

1 pound boneless, skinless
chicken breasts
sesame seeds, for sprinkling
red bell pepper, to garnish

For the Marinade
6 tablespoons vegetable oil
¼ cup tamari or soy sauce
¼ cup fresh lime juice
1-inch piece of fresh ginger, peeled and
chopped
3–4 garlic cloves
2 tablespoons light brown sugar
1 teaspoon Chinese-style chili sauce or
1 small red chili pepper, seeded and
chopped
2 tablespoons chopped fresh cilantro

For the Peanut Sauce
2 tablespoons smooth peanut butter
2 tablespoons soy sauce
1 tablespoon sesame or vegetable oil
2 scallions, chopped
2 garlic cloves
1–2 tablespoons fresh lime or lemon juice
1 tablespoon light brown sugar

Makes about 24

1 Prepare the marinade. Place all the marinade ingredients in the bowl of a food processor or blender and process until smooth and well blended, scraping down the sides of the bowl once. Pour into a shallow dish and set aside.

2 Put all the peanut sauce ingredients into the same food processor or blender, and process until well blended. If the sauce is too thick, add a little water and process again. Pour the sauce into a small bowl and cover until ready to serve.

3 Put the chicken breasts in the freezer for about 5 minutes to firm. On a cutting board, slice the chicken breasts in half horizontally, then cut them into thin strips. Cut the strips into ¾-inch pieces.

4 Add the chicken pieces to the marinade in the dish. Toss the chicken well to coat, cover with plastic wrap and marinate for 3–4 hours in a cool place, or overnight in the refrigerator.

5 Preheat the broiler. Line a baking sheet with foil and brush lightly with oil. Thread 2 or 3 pieces of marinated chicken onto skewers and sprinkle with the sesame seeds. Broil for 4–5 minutes or until golden, turning once. Serve with the peanut sauce and a garnish of red pepper strips.

Spicy Sun-dried Tomato Pizza Wedges

These spicy pizza wedges can be made with or without the pepperoni or sausage.

INGREDIENTS

3–4 tablespoons olive oil
2 onions, thinly sliced
2 garlic cloves, chopped
8 ounces mushrooms, sliced
1 can (8 ounces) chopped tomatoes
8 ounces pepperoni or cooked Italian-style
spicy sausage, chopped
1 teaspoon chili flakes
1 teaspoon dried oregano
½ cup sun-dried tomatoes, packed in oil,
drained and sliced
2 bottles (1 pound) marinated artichoke
hearts, well drained and cut into quarters
8 ounces mozzarella cheese, shredded
¼ cup freshly grated Parmesan cheese
fresh basil leaves, pitted black olives and
sliced fresh red bell pepper, to garnish

For the Dough
1 package pizza dough mix
cornmeal, for dusting
virgin olive oil, for brushing and drizzling

Makes 32

1 Prepare the pizza dough according to the manufacturer's instructions on the package. Set the prepared dough aside to rise for the required amount of time.

2 Prepare the tomato sauce. In a large, deep frying pan, heat the oil over medium-high heat. Add the sliced onions and cook for 3–5 minutes, or until softened. Add the chopped garlic and mushrooms and cook for 3–4 more minutes, or until the mushrooms begin to change color.

3 Stir in the chopped tomatoes, pepperoni, chili flakes and oregano and simmer for 20–30 minutes, stirring frequently, until the sauce is thickened and reduced. Stir in the sun-dried tomatoes and set the sauce aside to cool slightly.

4 Preheat the oven to 475°F. Line 1 large or 2 small baking sheets with foil, shiny side up. Sprinkle generously with cornmeal. Cut the dough in half and roll out each half to a 12-inch round. Transfer to the baking sheet and brush the dough with oil.

5 Divide the spicy tomato sauce between the dough rounds, spreading to within ½ inch of the edge. Bake for 5 minutes on the lowest shelf of the oven. Arrange half the artichoke hearts over each dough round, and sprinkle evenly with the mozzarella and a little Parmesan. Bake each one on the bottom shelf for 12–15 more minutes, or until the edge of the crust is crisp and brown and the topping is golden and bubbling. Transfer the pizza rounds to a wire rack, using a spatula, and let cool slightly.

6 Slide the pizzas onto a cutting board and cut each into 16 thin wedges. Garnish each pizza wedge with a basil leaf, one black olive and a slice of bell pepper and serve immediately.

BLINIS WITH SMOKED SALMON AND DILL CREAM

This recipe is perfect for New Year's Eve celebrations. The blinis go well with a glass of sparkling wine.

INGREDIENTS

scant 1 cup buckwheat flour
1 cup all-purpose flour
pinch of salt
1 tablespoon active dry yeast
2 eggs
1½ cups warm milk
1 tablespoon melted butter,
⅔ cup crème fraîche
3 tablespoons chopped fresh dill
8 ounces smoked salmon, thinly sliced
fresh dill sprigs, to garnish

Serves 4

1 Combine the flours and salt in a large bowl. Sprinkle in the yeast and mix. Separate one egg. Whisk the whole egg, the yolk (set aside the white), the warmed milk and the melted butter.

2 Pour the egg mixture onto the flour mixture. Beat well to form a smooth batter. Cover with plastic wrap and let rise for 1–2 hours.

3 Whisk the remaining egg white until it holds stiff peaks, and fold into the batter.

4 Preheat a heavy frying pan or griddle and brush with melted butter. Drop tablespoons of the batter onto the pan, spacing them well apart. Cook for about 40 seconds, or until bubbles appear on the surface.

5 Flip over the blinis and cook for 30 seconds on the other side. Wrap in foil and keep warm in the oven. Repeat with the remaining batter, buttering the pan each time.

6 Combine the crème fraîche and the chopped fresh dill. Serve the blinis topped with the slices of smoked salmon and the dill cream. Garnish each of the blinis with sprigs of fresh dill before serving.

PARMESAN FILO TRIANGLES

You can whip up these light and crunchy triangles at the last minute, using fresh or frozen sheets of filo pastry.

INGREDIENTS

3 large sheets filo pastry
olive oil, for brushing
3–4 tablespoons freshly grated Parmesan cheese
½ teaspoon crumbled dried thyme or sage

Makes about 24

COOK'S TIP

These will keep in an airtight container for up to three days, but handle carefully as they are very fragile. Reheat the triangles in a medium oven to crisp them up when you are ready to serve them.

1 Preheat the oven to 350°F. Line a large baking sheet with foil and brush lightly with oil. Lay one sheet of filo pastry on a work surface and brush lightly with a little olive oil. Sprinkle with half the Parmesan cheese and a little of the crumbled dried thyme or sage.

2 Cover with a second sheet of filo, brush with a little more oil and sprinkle with the remaining cheese and thyme or sage. Top with the remaining sheet of filo and brush very lightly with a little more oil. With a sharp knife, cut the filo-pastry stack in half lengthwise and then into squares. Cut each square into triangles.

3 Arrange the triangles on the baking sheet, scrunching them up slightly. Do not let them touch. Bake for 6–8 minutes, until crisp and golden. Cool slightly and serve immediately.

MINI FILLED BAKED POTATOES

Baked potatoes are always delicious, and the toppings can make them even more so: choose from luxurious

and extravagant ingredients, such as caviar and smoked salmon, and equally satisfying

but more everyday fare, such as cheese and baked beans.

INGREDIENTS

36 new potatoes, about 1½ inches in diameter, well scrubbed
1 cup thick sour cream
3–4 tablespoons snipped fresh chives
coarse salt, for sprinkling

Makes 36

VARIATION

If your guests are likely to be hungry, use medium-size potatoes. When cooked, cut in half, scoop out the flesh, mash with the other ingredients and spoon the mixture back into the skin. Serve warm.

COOK'S TIP

The potatoes can be baked in advance in the oven, then reheated in the microwave on high (100%) for 3–4 minutes.

2 To serve, make a cross in the top of each potato and squeeze gently to open. Make a hole in the center of each potato. Fill each one with sour cream, then sprinkle with the salt and the snipped chives. Serve immediately.

1 Preheat the oven to 350°F. Place the potatoes on a baking sheet and bake for 30–35 minutes or until the potatoes are tender when pierced with the tip of a sharp kitchen knife.

FILO CRACKERS

These festive-shaped sweet treats will make any party go with a bang! The crackers can be

prepared a day in advance, brushed with melted butter and kept covered with plastic wrap

in the fridge or freezer before baking.

INGREDIENTS

*1 package (10 ounces) frozen filo pastry,
thawed*
8 tablespoons (1 stick) butter, melted
thin foil ribbon, to decorate
sifted confectioners' sugar, to decorate

For the Filling
*1 pound apples, peeled, cored and finely
chopped*
1 teaspoon ground cinnamon
2 tablespoons light brown sugar
½ cup chopped pecans
1 cup fresh white bread crumbs
3 tablespoons golden raisins
3 heaping tablespoons currants

For the Lemon Sauce
⅔ cup superfine sugar
finely grated rind of 1 lemon
juice of 2 lemons

Makes about 24

2 Take one sheet of pastry at a time and cut it into 6 x 12-inch strips. Brush with butter. Place a spoonful of the filling at one end and fold in the sides, so the pastry measures 5 inches across. Brush the edges with butter and roll up. Pinch the "frill" tightly at either end of the cracker. Brush with melted butter.

4 To make the lemon sauce, put all the ingredients in a small saucepan and heat gently until all of the ingredients are dissolved, stirring occasionally. Pour the warm sauce into a sauceboat and serve with the filo crackers.

COOK'S TIP

*Make sure people know they
will be eating a sweet-filled cracker
by dredging the serving plate
with confectioners' sugar.*

1 Unwrap the filo pastry and cover it with plastic wrap and a damp cloth, to prevent it from drying out. Put the chopped apples in a large bowl and mix in the remaining filling ingredients.

3 Place the crackers on baking trays, cover and chill for 10 minutes. Preheat the oven to 375°F. Brush each cracker with melted butter. Bake the crackers for 35 minutes, or until they are golden brown. Let them cool slightly on the baking trays, then transfer to a wire rack to let cool completely. Add the ribbon for decoration.

Sablés with Goat Cheese and Strawberries

Sablés are little French cookies. They contrast well with the cheese and fruit in this recipe

and taste great served with a glass of chilled white wine.

Ingredients

6 tablespoons (¾ stick) butter, at room
temperature
1 generous cup flour
½ cup blanched hazelnuts, lightly toasted
and ground
2 tablespoons superfine sugar
2 egg yolks beaten with
2–3 tablespoons water
4 ounces goat cheese
4–6 large strawberries, cut into small
pieces
chopped hazelnuts, to decorate

Makes about 24

1 Make the pastry. Put the butter, flour, ground hazelnuts, sugar and beaten egg yolks in a food processor and process to make a smooth dough.

2 Place the dough on a sheet of plastic wrap and use the wrap to shape it into a log 1½ inches in diameter. Wrap and refrigerate overnight, until very firm.

3 Preheat the oven to 400°F and line a large baking sheet with parchment paper. Slice the dough into ¼-inch-thick rounds and arrange on the baking sheet. Bake for 7–10 minutes, or until golden brown. Remove to a wire rack to cool.

4 Crumble the cheese into pieces and mound a little on each sablé. Top with strawberry pieces and sprinkle with chopped hazelnuts. Serve warm.

Variation

*B*eat 4 ounces cream cheese with lemon zest and 1 tablespoon confectioners' sugar. Spread on top of the sablé and top with sliced fruits.

RICH CHOCOLATE AND FRUIT FONDUE

This sumptuous fruit fondue, with its rich, delicious sauce, makes a lavish finale to a party menu.

INGREDIENTS

*a selection of mixed fruit, such as
kumquats, apples, peaches and pears,
bananas, clementines, seedless grapes,
cherries, lychees, mango, papaya, figs,
plums and strawberries
lemon juice*

For the Chocolate
*8 ounces good-quality bittersweet
chocolate, chopped
2 tablespoons corn syrup
½ cup whipping cream
2–3 tablespoons brandy or
orange liqueur*

Makes 1½ cups

2 In a pan over low heat, combine the chocolate, corn syrup and cream. Stir until the chocolate is melted and smooth. Remove from the heat and stir in the brandy. Pour into a serving bowl and serve with the fruit.

1 On a cutting board, cut the kumquats, apples, peaches, pears and bananas into slices. Break the clementines into segments and peel the lychees, cube the mango and papaya and then cut the figs and plums into wedges. Leave the strawberries whole. Arrange the fruits in an attractive pattern on a large serving dish. Brush any cut-up fruit such as apples, pears or bananas with lemon juice to prevent the pieces from discoloring. Cover the dish with plastic wrap and refrigerate until ready to serve.

Stuffings, Sauces & Preserves

$\mathcal{S}$tuffings and sauces make up an essential part
of the Christmas fare, but they often require plenty of
preparation time. Many cooks find that, if they don't forget about
them altogether amid the hustle and bustle of the main events,
they decide against them as an optional extra. It is a good idea
to tackle as much as possible in advance when it comes to these
sides . Many of the recipes here improve with keeping and most
can be stored in the fridge or freezer until they are needed. In
the weeks leading up to Christmas, make the best use of the
seasonal produce available by bottling and preserving it in jars
for use throughout the festive weeks.

APRICOT AND RAISIN STUFFING

INGREDIENTS

3 tablespoons butter
1 large onion, sliced
1 cup dried apricots, soaked and drained
²⁄₃ cup raisins
juice and grated rind of 1 orange
1 apple, peeled, cored and chopped
2 cups fresh white bread crumbs
¼ teaspoon ground ginger
salt and freshly ground black pepper

Makes about 6 cups

1 Heat the butter in a small pan and fry the onion over medium heat until it is translucent.

2 Transfer the onion to a large mixing bowl and stir in the dried apricots, raisins, orange juice and rind, chopped apple, bread crumbs and ground ginger.

3 Season with salt and black pepper. Mix well with a wooden spoon, then let cool. Use the stuffing to pack the neck end of the turkey.

CHESTNUT STUFFING

INGREDIENTS

3 tablespoons butter
1 large onion, chopped
1 can (1 pound) unsweetened
chestnut purée
1 cup fresh white bread crumbs
3 tablespoons orange juice
grated nutmeg
½ teaspoon superfine sugar
salt and freshly ground black pepper

Makes about 4 cups

1 Heat the butter in a saucepan and fry the onion over medium heat for about 3 minutes, until it is translucent.

2 Remove the saucepan from the heat and mix the onion with the chestnut purée, bread crumbs, orange juice, grated nutmeg and sugar.

3 Season with salt and ground black pepper. Let cool. Use the stuffing to pack the neck end of the turkey.

CRANBERRY AND RICE STUFFING

INGREDIENTS

1¼ cups long-grain rice, washed and
drained
2½ cups chicken stock
4 tablespoons (½ stick) butter
1 large onion, chopped
1 cup cranberries
¼ cup orange juice
1 tablespoon chopped parsley
2 teaspoons chopped thyme
grated nutmeg
salt and freshly ground black pepper

Makes about 6 cups

1 Boil the rice and stock in a small pan. Cover and simmer for 15 minutes. Transfer the rice to a bowl and set aside. Heat the butter in a small pan and fry the onion. Add it to the rice.

2 Put the cranberries and orange juice in the cleaned pan and simmer until the fruit is tender. Transfer the fruit and any remaining juice into the rice.

3 Add the herbs and season. Let cool. Use to pack the turkey neck.

Clockwise from top: Chestnut Stuffing, Cranberry and Rice Stuffing, Apricot and Raisin Stuffing.

Apricot and Orange Stuffing

Ingredients

1 tablespoon butter
1 small onion, finely chopped
2 cups fresh bread crumbs
¼ cup finely chopped dried apricots
grated rind of ½ orange
1 small egg, beaten
1 tablespoon chopped fresh parsley
salt and freshly ground black pepper

Makes about 4 cups

1 Heat the butter in a frying pan and cook the onion gently until tender.

2 Let cool slightly and add the onion to the rest of the ingredients in a bowl.

3 Stir until thoroughly combined and season with plenty of salt and pepper.

Parsley, Lemon and Thyme Stuffing

Ingredients

2 cups fresh bread crumbs
2 tablespoons butter
1 tablespoon chopped fresh parsley
½ teaspoon dried thyme
grated rind of ¼ lemon
1 strip bacon, chopped
1 small egg, beaten
salt and freshly ground black pepper

Makes 2–3 cups

1 Combine all the ingredients in a large bowl and stir to combine them thoroughly.

Raisin and Nut Stuffing

Ingredients

2 cups fresh bread crumbs
⅓ cup raisins
½ cup walnuts, almonds, pistachios or pine nuts
1 tablespoon chopped fresh parsley
1 teaspoon chopped mixed herbs
1 small egg, beaten
2 tablespoons melted butter
salt and freshly ground black pepper

Makes about 4 cups

1 Combine all the ingredients thoroughly. Season well with plenty of salt and ground black pepper.

BREAD SAUCE

Smooth and surprisingly delicate, this old-fashioned sauce is traditionally served with roast

chicken, turkey and game birds. If you'd prefer a less strong flavor, reduce the number

of cloves and add a little freshly grated nutmeg instead.

INGREDIENTS

1 small onion
4 cloves
1 bay leaf
1¼ cups milk
2 cups fresh white bread crumbs
1 tablespoon butter
1 tablespoon light cream or half-and-half
salt and freshly ground black pepper

Serves 6

1 Peel the onion and stick the cloves into it. Put it into a saucepan with the bay leaf and pour in the milk.

2 Bring to a boil, then remove from the heat and steep for 15–20 minutes. Remove the bay leaf and onion.

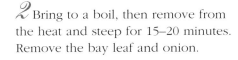

3 Return to the heat and stir in the bread crumbs. Simmer for 4–5 minutes, or until thick and creamy.

4 Stir in the butter and cream. Season with salt and pepper and serve.

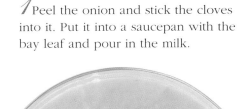

CRANBERRY SAUCE

This is a perfect sauce for roast turkey, but don't save it for festive occasions. The vibrant color and tart taste

are perfect partners to any white roast meat, and it makes a great addition to a chicken sandwich.

INGREDIENTS

1 orange
2 cups cranberries
1¼ cups sugar

Serves 6

1 Pare the rind thinly from the orange, taking care not to remove any white pith. Squeeze the juice.

2 Place the orange rind and juice in a saucepan with the cranberries, sugar and ⅔ cup water.

3 Bring to a boil, stirring until the sugar has dissolved, then simmer for 10–15 minutes, or until the berries burst.

4 Remove the rind. Cool before serving.

Tartar Sauce

This is an authentic tartar sauce to serve with all kinds of fish, but for a simpler version

you could always stir the flavorings into mayonnaise.

INGREDIENTS

2 hard-cooked eggs
1 egg yolk from a large egg
2 teaspoons lemon juice
¾ cup olive oil
1 teaspoon chopped capers
1 teaspoon chopped gherkins
1 teaspoon chopped fresh chives
1 teaspoon chopped fresh parsley
salt and white pepper

Serves 6

1 Halve the hard-cooked eggs, remove the yolks and press them through a strainer into a mixing bowl.

2 Using a spatula, blend in the raw yolk and mix thoroughly until smooth. Stir in the lemon juice.

3 Add the oil very slowly, a little at a time, whisking constantly. When it begins to thicken, add the oil more quickly to form a thick emulsion. Use a handheld mixer if you prefer.

4 Finely chop one egg white and stir into the sauce with the capers, gherkins and herbs. Season to taste. Serve as an accompaniment to fried or grilled fish.

Mousseline Sauce

This truly luscious sauce is subtly flavored, rich and creamy. Serve it as a dip with prepared

artichokes or artichoke hearts, or with fish or poultry.

INGREDIENTS

*1 batch Hollandaise sauce
or for a less rich sauce:
2 egg yolks
1 tablespoon lemon juice
6 tablespoons softened butter
6 tablespoons heavy cream
salt and freshly ground black pepper*

Serves 4

3 Using a large balloon whisk, whisk the heavy cream in a bowl. Continue to whisk the mixture until stiff peaks form.

4 Fold into the warm Hollandaise or prepared sauce and adjust the seasoning. You can add a little more lemon juice for extra tang.

1 If you are not using prepared Hollandaise, make the sauce. Whisk the yolks and lemon juice in a bowl over a pan of barely simmering water until very thick and fluffy.

2 Whisk in the softened butter, adding only a very little at a time; whisk well until it is thoroughly absorbed and the sauce has the consistency of mayonnaise.

Crème Anglaise

Here is the classic English custard. It is light and creamy, without the harsh flavors

or gaudy coloring of its poorer packaged relations. Serve hot or cold.

INGREDIENTS

1 vanilla pod
2 cups milk
3 tablespoons confectioners' sugar
4 egg yolks

Serves 4

> ### VARIATION
>
> *Steep a few strips of thinly pared*
> *lemon or orange rind with the milk,*
> *instead of the vanilla pod.*

1 Put the vanilla pod in a saucepan with the milk. Bring slowly to a boil. Remove from the heat and steep for 10 minutes before removing the pod.

2 Beat together the sugar and egg yolk until thick, light and creamy.

3 Slowly pour the warm milk onto the egg mixture, stirring constantly.

4 Place the bowl over a saucepan of hot water. Stir over low heat for 10 minutes, or until the mixture coats the back of the spoon. Remove from the heat immediately, as the custard will curdle if it is allowed to simmer.

5 Strain the custard into a pitcher if serving hot or, if serving cold, strain into a bowl and cover the surface with buttered waxed paper or plastic wrap.

CUMBERLAND RUM BUTTER

No Christmas dinner would be complete without a traditional Christmas pudding to round it off.

This rich and luscious rum butter is the perfect accompaniment.

INGREDIENTS

*16 tablespoons (2 sticks) unsalted butter
at room temperature
1 cup light brown sugar
6 tablespoons dark rum, or to taste*

Makes about 1 pound

1 Beat the butter and sugar until the mixture is soft, creamy and pale in color. Gradually add the rum, almost drop by drop, beating to incorporate each addition before adding more. If you are too hasty in adding the rum, the mixture may curdle.

2 When all the rum has been added, spoon the mixture into a covered container and chill for at least 1 hour. The butter will keep well in the fridge for about 4 weeks.

VARIATION

A variety of liqueurs can be added to the butter and sugar to make delicious alternative accompaniments. Try the recipe with brandy or an orange-flavored liqueur.

Savory Butters

This selection of eight tiny pots of unusual flavored butters can be used as garnishes for meat,

fish and vegetables, as a topping for canapés or as a tasty addition to sauces.

INGREDIENTS

1 pound (4 sticks) unsalted butter
2 tablespoons Stilton
3 anchovy fillets
1 teaspoon curry paste
1 garlic clove, crushed
2 teaspoons finely chopped fresh tarragon
1 tablespoon creamed horseradish
1 tablespoon chopped fresh parsley
1 teaspoon grated lime rind
¼ teaspoon chili sauce

Makes about ¼ cup
of each flavor

1 Place the butter in a food processor. Process until light and fluffy. Divide the butter into 8 portions.

2 Crumble the Stilton and combine with a portion of butter. Pound the anchovies to a paste with a mortar and pestle and mix with the second portion of butter. Stir the curry paste into the third and the crushed garlic into the fourth portion.

3 Stir the tarragon into the fifth portion and the creamed horseradish into the sixth portion. Add the parsley and the lime rind to the seventh portion, and to the last portion add the chili sauce. Pack each flavored butter into a tiny sterilized jar with a lid and label clearly. Store in the fridge.

> ### COOK'S TIP
> *Make up a whole batch of these butters and freeze them. They will keep unopened in the freezer for up to 3 months. Once opened, consume within 3 days.*

Anchovy Spread

This delicious spread has an intense, concentrated flavor and is best served with plain toast.

INGREDIENTS

*2 cans (2 ounces each) anchovy
fillets in olive oil
4 garlic cloves, crushed
2 egg yolks
2 tablespoons red wine vinegar
1¼ cups olive oil
¼ teaspoon freshly ground black pepper
2 tablespoons chopped fresh basil or thyme*

Makes 2½ cups

1 Drain the oil from the anchovies and reserve. Place the anchovies and garlic in a food processor. Process until smooth. Add the egg yolks and vinegar, and process until the egg and vinegar have been absorbed by the anchovies.

2 Measure the oil into a measuring cup and add the reserved anchovy oil. Set the food processor on a low speed and gradually add the oil, drop by drop, to the anchovy mixture, until it is thick and smooth.

3 Add some freshly ground black pepper and the chopped fresh herbs, and blend well until the mixture is smooth. Spoon the mixture into small sterilized jars with lids, seal with a waxed-paper disk, cover with the lid, and label with the name of the spread and the date it was made. Store the unopened jars of spread in the fridge until they are needed.

Christmas Chutney

This chutney makes the perfect accompaniment to cold meats, pâtés and cheese. It has a sweet

but spicy flavor. Other fruits, such as quince, green plums or rhubarb may used instead.

INGREDIENTS

9 plums, pitted
6 pears, peeled and cored
2 apples, peeled and cored
4 celery stalks
1 pound onions, sliced
1 pound tomatoes, skinned
½ cup raisins
1 tablespoon grated fresh ginger
2 tablespoons pickling spice
3¾ cups cider vinegar
2 cups granulated sugar

Makes 4½ pounds

1 Chop the plums, pears, apples, celery and onions and cut the tomatoes into quarters. Place all these ingredients with the raisins and ginger in a very large saucepan.

2 Spoon the pickling spice onto a square of clean, fine cheesecloth and tie with string to secure. Add to the saucepan of fruit and vegetables along with half the vinegar and bring to a boil, stirring. Cook for 2 hours.

3 Meanwhile, sterilize the jars and lids you will need. When all the ingredients are tender, stir in the remaining vinegar and the sugar. Boil until thick, remove the bag of spices and fill each jar with chutney. Cover with a waxed-paper disk and plastic lid, and label when cool.

COOK'S TIP

Once opened, this chutney will keep for up to one week in a resealable jar. If you wish, add attractive ribbons, tags and labels and give to a friend as a special Christmas gift.

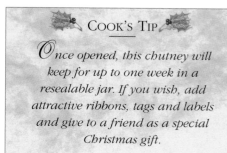

Piccalilli

The piquancy of this relish partners well with sausages, as well as with most bacon or ham dishes.

INGREDIENTS

1½ pounds cauliflower
1 pound small onions
12 ounces green beans
1 teaspoon ground turmeric
1 teaspoon dry mustard powder
2 teaspoons cornstarch
2½ cups vinegar

Makes three 1-pound jars

1 Cut the cauliflower into tiny florets.

2 Peel the onions and trim the green beans.

3 In a small saucepan, measure out the turmeric, mustard powder and cornstarch. Pour the vinegar into the saucepan. Stir well and simmer for 10 minutes over low heat.

4 Pour the vinegar mixture over the vegetables in a large saucepan, mix well and simmer for 45 minutes.

5 Pour into sterilized jars. Seal each jar with a wax disk and a tight-fitting cellophane top. Store in a cool, dark place. The piccalilli will keep well, unopened, for up to a year. Once opened, store in the fridge and consume within a week.

Tomato Chutney

This spicy chutney is delicious with a selection of cheeses and crackers, or with cold meats.

INGREDIENTS

2 pounds tomatoes
1⅓ cups raisins
8 ounces onions, chopped
1 cup superfine sugar
2½ cups malt vinegar

Makes three 1-pound jars

1 Put the tomatoes in a bowl and pour boiling water over them. Leave the tomatoes immersed in the water for 30 seconds, then remove with a slotted spoon and plunge them into cold water. Peel the tomatoes and chop roughly. Put in a preserving pan.

2 Add the raisins, chopped onions and superfine sugar.

3 Pour in the vinegar. Bring to a boil and let simmer, uncovered, for 2 hours. Pour into sterilized jars. Seal with a wax disk and cover with a tight-fitting cellophane top. Store in a cool, dark place. The chutney will keep well, unopened, for up to a year. Once opened, store in the fridge and consume within a week.

QUINCE PASTE

This paste is known in Spain as pasta de membrillo. *It is decorated with confectioners' sugar and sometimes cloves, and served after meals or to decorate desserts. If you can't find quinces, try using fresh apricots or even cranberries.*

INGREDIENTS

2¼ pounds quinces
4 cups water
4¼ cups superfine sugar
vegetable oil, for brushing
confectioners' sugar, for dusting
whole cloves, to decorate

Makes about 2½ pounds

COOK'S TIP

If you would like to pack this tangy paste as a gift, layer it in a box between sheets of parchment paper.

1 Wash and slice the quinces and put them in a large pan with the water. Bring to a boil, then simmer for about 45 minutes, until the fruit is soft.

2 Mash the fruit against the sides of the pan, then spoon it and the liquid into a jelly bag suspended over a large bowl. Let drain for at least 2 hours, without squeezing the bag.

3 Pour the strained juice into the cleaned pan, add the sugar and stir over low heat to dissolve. Cook over low heat for about 2 hours, stirring frequently, until a spoon drawn through the paste parts it into 2 sections.

4 Lightly brush a jelly-roll pan with oil, pour in the paste and let set. When it is cool, cut it into diamonds or other shapes, dust with confectioners' sugar and stud each piece with a clove. Store between layers of parchment paper in an airtight container.

CRAB-APPLE AND LAVENDER JELLY

This fragrant, clear jelly can be made in the months before Christmas and stored until needed.

INGREDIENTS

5 cups crab apples
7½ cups water
lavender stems
4 cups granulated sugar

Makes about 2 pounds

1 Cut the crab apples into chunks and place in a large pan with the water and 2 stems of lavender. Bring to a boil, then cover the pan and simmer very gently for 1 hour, stirring occasionally, until the fruit is pulpy.

2 Suspend a jelly bag over a large bowl. Sterilize the jelly bag by pouring some boiling water through it. When the bowl is full of water, discard the water and replace the jelly bag over the bowl.

3 Slowly pour the pulped fruit mixture from the saucepan into the jelly bag. Let the juice from the mixture drip slowly through for several hours. Do not try to speed up the straining process by squeezing the bag, or the jelly will become cloudy.

4 Discard the pulp and measure the quantity of juice in the bowl. To each 2½ cups of juice add 2 cups of sugar and pour into a clean pan. Sterilize the jars and lids required.

5 Heat the juice gently, stirring occasionally, until the sugar has dissolved. Bring to a boil and boil rapidly for 8–10 minutes, until setting point has been reached. When tested, the temperature should be 221°F. If you don't have a candy thermometer, put a small amount of jelly on a cold plate and let cool. The surface should wrinkle when you push the jelly. If not yet set, continue to boil and then retest.

6 Remove from the heat and skim off any froth from the surface. Pour the jelly into the warm sterilized jars. Dip the lavender in boiling water and insert a stem into each jar. Cover with a disk of wax and then with cellophane and attached with a rubber band.

Apple and Mint Jelly

This jelly tastes delicious served with freshly cooked vegetables.

It is also makes a traditional accompaniment to rich roasted meats such as lamb.

INGREDIENTS

2 pounds apples
granulated sugar
3 tablespoons chopped fresh mint

Makes three 1-pound jars

1 Chop the apples roughly and put them in a preserving pan.

2 Add enough water to cover the apples. Simmer until the fruit is soft.

3 Suspend a jelly bag over a bowl. Pour the mixture through the bag, letting it drip overnight. Do not squeeze the bag.

4 Measure the amount of juice that drains from the jelly bag. To every 2½ cups of juice, add 2¾ cups granulated sugar. Stir the sugar into the juice.

5 Place the juice and sugar in a large saucepan and warm over low heat, stirring continuously. Dissolve the sugar in the juice and then increase the heat and bring the liquid to a boil. Test for setting by pouring about 1 tablespoon onto a cold plate and letting it cool. If a wrinkle forms on the surface when pushed with a fingertip, the jelly is almost set. When a set is reached, let the jelly cool.

6 Stir in the chopped mint and pour into sterilized jars. Seal each jar with a wax disk and a tight-fitting cellophane top. Store in a cool, dark place. The jelly will keep, unopened, for up to a year. Once opened, keep in the fridge and consume within a week.

POACHED SPICED PLUMS IN BRANDY

Bottling spiced fruit is a great way to preserve summer flavors for eating in winter.

Serve these spiced plums as a dessert, with freshly whipped cream, if desired.

INGREDIENTS

2½ cups brandy
rind of 1 lemon, peeled in a long strip
1⅔ cups superfine sugar
1 cinnamon stick
2 pounds fresh plums

Makes 2 pounds

VARIATION

Other fruits that can be preserved successfully in this way include fresh pears and peaches.

1 Put the brandy, sugar and cinnamon stick in a large pan and heat gently to dissolve the sugar. Add the plums and lemon rind. Poach for 15 minutes, or until soft. Remove with a slotted spoon.

2 Reduce the syrup by a third by rapid boiling. Strain it over the plums. Bottle the plums in large, sterilized jars. Seal tightly and store for up to 6 months in a cool, dark place.

Spiced Pickled Pears

These delicious pears are the perfect accompaniment for cooked ham or cold meat salads.

INGREDIENTS

2 pounds pears
2½ cups white wine vinegar
1 cup superfine sugar
1 cinnamon stick
5 star anise
10 whole cloves

Makes 2 pounds

COOK'S TIP

The pears will keep for up to a year unopened. Once opened, store in the fridge and consume within one week.

1 Use a sharp knife to peel the pears, keeping them whole and leaving the flesh on the stalks. Heat the white wine vinegar and superfine sugar together in a saucepan, stirring continuously, until the sugar has melted. Pour the liquid over the pears and poach for 15 minutes.

2 Add the cinnamon stick, star anise and cloves and simmer for 10 minutes. Remove the pears and pack tightly into sterilized jars. Simmer the syrup for another 15 minutes and strain it over the pears. Seal the jars tightly and store in a cool, dark place.

Desserts

*C*hristmas is a time to indulge in desserts.
At Christmas Dinner, most guests will expect Traditional
Christmas Pudding, but other variations on the festive theme,
such as Chocolate and Chestnut Yule Log or Christmas
Cranberry Bombe, will be just as welcome. After a heavy meal,
a fruit-based dessert such as Ruby Fruit Salad or Spiced Pears in
Red Wine will always be appreciated and, for successful
entertaining, try individual desserts, such as sinful Frozen
Grand Marnier Soufflés laced with alcohol. Specialities for
chocaholics include Amaretto Mousses with Chocolate Sauce,
while Chocolate Crêpes with Plums and Port will provide a
sophisticated end to any main course.

GINGER TRIFLE

This is a good way to use up leftover cake, whether plain, chocolate or gingerbread. You can substitute

honey for the ginger and corn syrup, if desired. This dessert can be made the day before serving.

INGREDIENTS

8 good-sized portions gingerbread or
· other cake
¼ cup Grand Marnier or sherry
2 ripe pears, peeled, cored and cubed
2 bananas, thickly sliced
2 oranges, segmented
1 or 2 pieces ginger, finely chopped,
2 tablespoons corn syrup

For the Custard
2 eggs
¼ cup superfine sugar
1 tablespoon cornstarch
2 cups milk
few drops of vanilla extract

To Decorate
⅔ cup heavy cream, lightly whipped
¼ cup chopped almonds, toasted
4 candied cherries
8 small pieces angelica

Serves 8

3 Mix all the fruit with the ginger and corn syrup. Spoon into the bowl on top of the gingerbread. Spoon on the custard to cover and chill until set.

4 Cover the top of the trifle with whipped cream and scatter the almonds over the cream. Arrange the candied cherries and angelica around the edge.

1 Cut the gingerbread into 1½-inch cubes. Put them in the bottom of a 7½-cup glass bowl. Sprinkle on the liqueur and set aside.

2 For the custard, whisk the eggs, sugar and cornstarch into a pan with a little milk. Heat the remaining milk until almost boiling. Pour it onto the egg mixture, whisking. Heat, stirring, until thickened. Simmer for 2 minutes. Add the vanilla extract and let cool.

Ruby Fruit Salad

After a rich main course, this port-flavored fruit salad is light and refreshing.

You can use any fruit that is available.

Ingredients

1¼ cups water
½ cup superfine sugar
1 cinnamon stick
4 cloves
pared rind of 1 orange
1¼ cups port
2 oranges
1 small ripe honeydew melon
4 small bananas
2 apples
1 small bunch seedless grapes

Serves 8

3 On a cutting board, cut the melon in half, remove the seeds and scoop out the flesh with a melon baller or cut it into small cubes. Add it to the syrup. Peel the bananas and cut them into ½-inch slices.

4 Quarter and core the apples and cut them into small cubes. (Leave the skin on, or peel if the skin is tough.) Halve the grapes if large, or leave them whole. Stir all the fruit into the syrup, cover and chill for an hour before serving.

1 Put the water, sugar, spices and pared orange rind in a saucepan and stir over low heat, to dissolve the sugar. Then bring the liquid to a boil, cover the pan with a lid and let simmer gently for 10 minutes. Remove the pan from the heat and set aside to cool, then add the port.

2 Strain the liquid through a sieve into a mixing bowl, to remove the spices and orange rind. With a sharp knife, cut off all the skin and pith from the oranges. Then, holding each orange over the bowl to catch the juice, cut away the segments by slicing between the membrane that divides each segment and letting the segments drop into the syrup. Squeeze the remaining pith to release as much of the remaining juice as possible.

GOLDEN GINGER COMPOTE

Warm, spicy and full of sun-ripened ingredients—this is the perfect Christmas dessert.

INGREDIENTS

2 cups kumquats
1¼ cups dried apricots
2 tablespoons raisins
1⅔ cups water
1 orange
1-inch piece fresh ginger, peeled and grated
4 cardamom pods, crushed
4 cloves
2 tablespoons honey
1 tablespoon slivered almonds, toasted

Serves 4

1 Wash the kumquats and, if they are large, cut them in half. Place them in a pan with the apricots, raisins and water. Bring to a boil.

2 Pare the rind from the orange and add to the pan. Add the ginger, the cardamom pods and the cloves.

3 Reduce the heat, cover and simmer for about 30 minutes, or until the fruit is tender, stirring occasionally.

4 Squeeze the orange juice and add to the pan with honey to sweeten. Sprinkle with almonds and serve.

COOK'S TIP

You can use ready-to-eat dried apricots. Reduce the liquid to 1¼ cups, and add the apricots for the last 5 minutes.

SPICED PEARS IN RED WINE

Serve these pears hot or cold, with lightly whipped cream. The flavors improve over

time, so you can make this several days before you want to serve it.

INGREDIENTS

2½ cups red wine
1 cup superfine sugar
cinnamon stick
6 cloves
finely grated rind of 1 orange
2 teaspoons grated ginger
8 even-size firm pears, with stalks
1 tablespoon brandy
2 tablespoons almonds toasted or
hazelnuts, to decorate

Serves 8

3 Remove the pears from the syrup using a slotted spoon, being careful not to pull out the stalks. Put the pears in one large serving bowl or 8 individual bowls.

4 Bring the syrup to a boil and boil it rapidly until it thickens and reduces. Let cool slightly, add the brandy and strain over the pears. Scatter the toasted nuts on top, to decorate.

1 Choose a pan large enough to hold all the pears upright in one layer. Put all the ingredients except the pears, brandy and almonds in the pan and heat slowly until the sugar has dissolved. Simmer for 5 minutes.

2 Peel the pears, leaving the stalks on, and cut away the flower end. Arrange them upright in the pan. Cover with a lid and simmer until the pears are tender. The cooking time will depend on their size, but will be about 45 minutes.

Stuffed Peaches with Mascarpone Cream

Mascarpone is a thick, velvety Italian cream cheese, made from cow's milk.

Although it can be used as a thickening agent in savory recipes, it is often used

in desserts or eaten with a variety of fresh fruit.

INGREDIENTS

4 large peaches, halved and pitted
1½ ounces amaretti cookies, crumbled
2 tablespoons ground almonds
3 tablespoons sugar
1 tablespoon cocoa powder
⅔ cup sweet white wine
2 tablespoons butter

For the Mascarpone Cream
2 tablespoons superfine sugar
3 egg yolks
1 tablespoon sweet white wine
1 cup mascarpone cheese
⅔ cup heavy cream

Serves 4

2 Combine the amaretti, ground almonds, sugar, cocoa and peach flesh. Add enough wine to make the mixture into a thick paste.

3 Place the halved peaches in a buttered ovenproof dish and fill them with the stuffing. Dot each peach with the butter, then pour the remaining wine into the dish. Bake for 35 minutes.

4 To make the mascarpone cream, beat the sugar and egg yolks until thick and pale. Stir in the wine, then fold in the mascarpone. Whip the heavy cream to form soft peaks and fold into the mixture. Remove the peaches from the oven and let cool. Serve the peaches at room temperature, with the mascarpone.

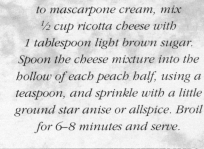

> ### VARIATION
>
> *As a low-fat alternative to mascarpone cream, mix ½ cup ricotta cheese with 1 tablespoon light brown sugar. Spoon the cheese mixture into the hollow of each peach half, using a teaspoon, and sprinkle with a little ground star anise or allspice. Broil for 6–8 minutes and serve.*

1 Preheat the oven to 400°F. Using a teaspoon, scoop some of the flesh from the cavities in the peaches, to make a space for stuffing. Chop up the scooped-out flesh with a knife.

CRÊPES WITH ORANGE SAUCE

This is a sophisticated dessert that is easy to make at home. You can make

the crêpes in advance; you will be able to put the dish together quickly at the last minute.

INGREDIENTS

⅔ cup flour
¼ teaspoon salt
2 tablespoons superfine sugar
2 eggs, lightly beaten
1 cup milk
¼ cup water
2 tablespoons orange flower water or
orange liqueur (optional)
2 tablespoons unsalted butter, melted, plus
more for frying

For the Orange Sauce
6 tablespoons unsalted butter
¼ cup superfine sugar
grated rind and juice of 1 large
unwaxed orange
grated rind and juice of
1 unwaxed lemon
⅔ cup fresh orange juice
¼ cup orange liqueur
brandy and orange liqueur, for flaming
(optional)
orange segments, to decorate

Serves 6

2 Heat an 8-inch crêpe pan (preferably nonstick) over medium heat. Stir the melted butter into the crêpe batter. Brush the hot pan with a little extra melted butter and pour in about 2 tablespoons of batter. Quickly tilt and rotate the pan to cover the bottom with a thin layer of batter. Cook for about 1 minute, until the top is set and the base is golden. With a spatula, lift the edge to check the color, then carefully turn over the crêpe and cook for 20–30 seconds, just to set. Transfer to a plate.

4 To make the sauce, melt the butter in a large frying pan over medium-low heat, then stir in the sugar, orange and lemon rind and juice, the additional orange juice and the orange liqueur, if using.

5 Place a crêpe in the pan browned side down, swirling gently to coat with the sauce. Fold it in half, then in half again to form a triangle, and push to the side of the pan. Continue heating and folding the crêpes until all are warm and covered with the sauce.

1 Sift together the flour, salt and sugar. Make a well in the center and pour in the eggs. Beat the eggs, whisking in the flour until it is all incorporated. Whisk in the milk and water until smooth. Whisk in the orange flower water or liqueur. Then strain the batter into a bowl and set aside.

3 Continue cooking the crêpes, stirring the batter occasionally and brushing the pan with a little melted butter when necessary. Place a sheet of plastic wrap between each crêpe as they are stacked to prevent sticking. (Crêpes can be prepared ahead to this point—wrap and chill until ready to use.)

6 If you want to flame the crêpes, heat 2–3 tablespoons each of orange liqueur and brandy in a small saucepan over medium heat. Remove the pan from the heat, carefully ignite the liquid with a match, then gently pour it over the crêpes. Scatter the orange segments on top and serve immediately.

Mini Millefeuille

This pâtisserie classic is a delectable combination of tender puff pastry sandwiched with luscious pastry cream. It is difficult to cut, making individual servings a brilliant solution.

INGREDIENTS

1 pound puff pastry
6 egg yolks
⅓ cup superfine sugar
3 tablespoons flour
1½ cups milk
2 tablespoons kirsch or cherry liqueur
(optional)
3 cups raspberries
confectioners' sugar, for dusting
strawberry or raspberry coulis, to serve

Serves 8

1 Lightly butter two large baking sheets and then sprinkle them very lightly with cold water.

2 On a lightly floured surface, roll out the pastry to a ⅛-inch thickness. Using a 4-inch cutter, cut out 12 rounds. Place on the baking sheets and prick with a fork. Chill for 30 minutes. Preheat the oven to 400°F.

3 Bake the pastry rounds for 15–20 minutes, or until golden, then transfer to wire racks to cool.

4 Whisk the egg yolks and sugar until light and creamy, then whisk in the flour until blended. Bring the milk to a boil and pour it over the egg mixture, whisking. Return to the saucepan, bring to a boil and boil for 2 minutes, whisking. Remove the pan from the heat and whisk in the kirsch. Pour into a bowl and press plastic wrap on the surface to prevent a skin from forming. Set aside to cool.

5 To assemble, split the pastry rounds in half. Spread one round at a time with a little pastry cream. Arrange a layer of raspberries over the cream and top with a second pastry round. Spread with a little more cream and a few more raspberries. Top with a third pastry round, flat side up. Dust with confectioners' sugar and serve with the coulis.

RED FRUIT FILO BASKETS

This elegant dessert looks very festive. The Filo Baskets are low in fat and need only a fine brushing of oil

before baking. A light oil such as sunflower is the best choice for this recipe.

INGREDIENTS

3 sheets filo pastry (about 3½ ounces)
1 tablespoon sunflower oil
1½ cups red currants
1 cup strained plain yogurt
1 teaspoon confectioners' sugar
1 cup whole strawberries and raspberries,
to decorate

Serves 6

1 Preheat the oven to 400°F. Using a sharp kitchen knife, cut the sheets of filo pastry into 18 squares with sides about 4 inches long.

2 Brush each filo square lightly with oil, then arrange the squares to overlap in six small tartlet pans, layering them in threes. Bake for 6–8 minutes, until crisp and golden. Remove the baskets from the tartlet pans using a spatula, and let them cool.

3 Reserve a few sprigs of red currants to add to the decoration and string the rest through the tines of a fork. Stir the currants into the yogurt.

4 Spoon the yogurt into the filo baskets. Decorate the baskets with the red fruits and sprinkle them lightly with confectioners' sugar.

CRUNCHY APPLE AND ALMOND TART

Do not be tempted to add any sugar to the apples, as this makes them produce too

much liquid. All the sweetness you'll need is in the pastry and topping.

INGREDIENTS

6 tablespoons butter
1½ cups flour
scant ⅓ cup ground almonds
2 tablespoons superfine sugar
1 egg yolk
1 tablespoon cold water
¼ teaspoon almond extract
sifted confectioners' sugar, to decorate

For the Crunchy Topping
1 cup flour
¼ teaspoon pumpkin pie spice
4 tablespoons (½ stick) butter, cubed
¼ cup sugar
½ cup slivered almonds

For the filling
1½ pounds apples
2 tablespoons raisins

Serves 8

1 To make the pastry, rub the butter into the flour, either with your fingertips in a large mixing bowl or in a food processor, until it resembles fine bread crumbs. Stir in the ground almonds and sugar. Whisk the egg yolk, water and almond extract together and mix them into the dry ingredients to form a soft, pliable dough. Knead the dough lightly until smooth, wrap in plastic wrap and let sit in a cool place or in the fridge to rest for about 20 minutes.

2 Meanwhile, make the crunchy topping. Sift the flour and pumpkin pie spice into a bowl and rub in the butter. Stir in the sugar and almonds.

3 Roll out the pastry on a lightly floured surface and use it to line a 9-inch springform pan, taking care to press it neatly into the edges and to make a lip around the top edge.

4 Remove the excess pastry to neaten the edge. Let chill in the fridge for about 15 minutes.

5 Preheat the oven to 375°F. Place a baking sheet in the oven to preheat. Peel, core and slice the apples thinly. Arrange the slices on the pastry in overlapping concentric circles, doming the center. Scatter the raisins on top. The tart will seem too full at this stage, but as the apples cook the filling will drop slightly.

6 Cover the apples with the crunchy topping mixture, pressing it on lightly. Bake on the hot baking sheet for 25–30 minutes, or until the top is golden brown and the apples are tender (test them with a fine skewer). Let the tart cool in the pan for 10 minutes before removing. The tart can be served either warm or cool, dusted with sifted confectioners' sugar.

MANGO AND AMARETTI STRUDEL

Fresh mango and crushed amaretti wrapped in wafer-thin filo pastry make a

seasonal treat that is equally delicious made with apricots or plums.

INGREDIENTS

1 large mango
grated rind of 1 lemon
2 amaretti cookies
3 tablespoons light brown sugar
¼ cup whole-wheat bread crumbs
2 filo pastry sheets
2 tablespoons (¼ stick) margarine,
melted
1 tablespoon chopped almonds
confectioners' sugar, for dusting

Serves 4

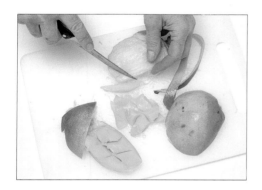

1 Preheat the oven to 375°F. Lightly grease a large baking sheet. Halve, pit and peel the mango. Cut the flesh into cubes, then place them in a bowl and sprinkle with the grated lemon rind.

2 Crush the amaretti cookies with a rolling pin and mix them with the brown sugar and the whole-wheat bread crumbs.

3 Lay one sheet of filo on a flat surface and brush with a quarter of the melted margarine. Top with the second sheet, brush with one-third of the remaining margarine, then fold both sheets over, if necessary, to make a rectangle measuring 11 x 9½ inches. Brush the rectangle with half the remaining margarine.

4 Sprinkle the filo with the amaretti mixture, leaving a 2-inch border on each long side. Arrange the mango cubes over the top.

5 Roll up the filo from one of the long sides, jelly-roll fashion. Lift the strudel onto the baking sheet, seam side down. Brush with the remaining melted margarine and sprinkle with the chopped almonds.

6 Bake the strudel for 20–25 minutes, until golden brown, then carefully transfer it to a board. Dust the strudel with the confectioners' sugar, slice diagonally and serve warm.

COOK'S TIP

The easiest way to prepare a mango is to cut horizontally through the fruit, keeping the knife blade close to the pit. Repeat on the other side of the pit and peel off the skin. Remove the remaining skin and flesh from around the pit.

TRADITIONAL CHRISTMAS PUDDING

This recipe makes enough to fill one large mold or two small pudding molds or bowls.

It can be made up to a month before Christmas and stored in a cool, dry place.

Steam the pudding for 2 hours before serving. Serve topped with a decorative sprig of holly.

INGREDIENTS

8 tablespoons (1 stick) butter
1 cup dark brown sugar
½ cup self-rising flour
1 teaspoon pumpkin pie spice
¼ teaspoon nutmeg
½ teaspoon ground cinnamon
2 eggs
2 cups fresh white bread crumbs
1 cup golden raisins
1 cup raisins
½ cup currants
3 tablespoons chopped mixed citrus peel
¼ cup chopped almonds
1 small apple, peeled, cored and coarsely grated
finely grated rind of 1 orange or lemon
juice of 1 orange or lemon, made up to ⅔ cup with brandy, rum or sherry

Serves 8

1 Cut a disk of waxed paper to fit the bottom of the mold, and butter the disk and mold.

2 Whisk the butter and sugar together until soft. Beat in the flour, spices and eggs. Mix in the remaining ingredients thoroughly. The batter should have a soft, dropping consistency.

3 Transfer the batter to the greased mold and level the top.

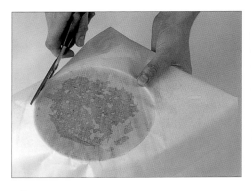

4 Cover with another disk of buttered waxed paper.

5 Make a pleat across the center of a large piece of waxed paper and cover the mold, tying it with string. Pleat a piece of foil in the same way and cover the mold, tucking it under the waxed-paper frill.

6 Tie another piece of string around the mold and across the top, as a handle. Place the mold in a steamer over a pan of simmering water and steam for 6 hours. Alternatively, put the mold in a large pan, pour in enough boiling water to come halfway up the sides of the mold and cover the pan with a tight-fitting lid. Check that the water is simmering and add boiling water as it evaporates. When the pudding(s) has cooked, let cool completely. Then remove the foil and waxed paper. Wipe the mold clean and replace the waxed paper and foil with clean pieces, ready for reheating.

TO SERVE

Steam for 2 hours. Upend onto a plate and let stand for 5 minutes before removing the pudding basin. (The steam will rise to the top of the mold and help to loosen the pudding.)

CHOCOLATE AND CHESTNUT YULE LOG

This chocolate log is traditionally served at Christmas. Make it the day before it is needed

or some time in advance and freeze it. It makes an excellent dessert for a party.

INGREDIENTS

2 tablespoons flour
2 tablespoons cocoa powder
pinch of salt
3 large eggs, separated
large pinch cream of tartar
½ cup superfine sugar
2–3 drops almond extract
sifted cocoa powder and holly sprigs,
to decorate

For the Filling
1 tablespoon rum or brandy
½ envelope (1 teaspoon) powdered gelatin
4 ounces unsweetened chocolate, broken
into squares
¼ cup superfine sugar
1 can (8 ounces) chestnut purée
1¼ cups heavy cream

Serves 8

1 Preheat the oven to 350°F. Grease and line a 9 x 13-inch jelly-roll pan and line the base with parchment paper. Sift the flour, cocoa and salt together onto a piece of waxed paper.

2 Put the egg whites in a large clean bowl and whisk them until frothy. Add the cream of tartar and whisk until stiff. Gradually whisk in half the sugar, until the mixture will stand in stiff peaks.

3 Put the egg yolks and the remaining sugar in another bowl and whisk until thick and pale. Add the almond extract. Stir in the sifted flour and cocoa mixture. Last, fold in the egg whites, using a metal spoon, until everything is evenly blended. Be careful not to overmix.

4 Transfer the mixture to the prepared jelly-roll pan and level the top. Bake for 15–20 minutes, or until springy to the touch. Have ready a large piece of waxed paper dusted liberally with superfine sugar. Transfer the jelly roll to the paper, remove the parchment paper, and roll it up with the waxed paper still inside. Let cool completely on a wire rack.

5 Put the rum or brandy in a cup and sprinkle on the gelatin; let become spongy. Melt the chocolate in a 2½-cup bowl over a pan of hot water. Melt the gelatin over barely simmering water and add to the chocolate. With an electric beater, whisk in the sugar and chestnut purée. Remove from the heat and let cool. Whisk the cream until it holds soft peaks. Fold the two mixtures together evenly.

6 Unroll the jelly roll carefully, spread it with half the filling and roll it up again. Place it on a serving dish and spread on the rest of the chocolate cream to cover it. Mark it with a fork to resemble a log. Chill until firm. Dust the cake with sifted cocoa powder and decorate around the edges of the plate with sprigs of holly.

Frozen Grand Marnier Soufflés

These luxurious puddings are always appreciated and make a wonderful end to any Christmastime meal.

INGREDIENTS

1 cup superfine sugar
6 large eggs, separated
1 cup milk
1 envelope (½ ounce) powdered gelatin,
soaked in 3 tablespoons cold water
2 cups heavy cream
¼ cup Grand Marnier

Serves 8

1 Fold a double collar of waxed paper around each of eight ramekins and tie with string. (You could make one large soufflé if desired.) Put 6 tablespoons of the superfine sugar in a large mixing bowl with the egg yolks and whisk until the yolks are pale. This will take about 5 minutes by hand and about 3 minutes if you use a handheld mixer.

2 Heat the milk until almost boiling and pour it onto the yolks, whisking constantly. Return to the pan and stir over low heat until it is thick enough to coat the back of the spoon. Remove the pan from the heat. Stir the soaked gelatin into the custard. Pour into a bowl and let cool. Whisk occasionally, until the custard is on the point of setting.

3 Put the remaining sugar in a pan with the water and dissolve it over low heat. Bring to a boil and boil rapidly until the mixture reaches the soft ball stage, or 238°F on a candy thermometer. Remove from the heat. In a clean bowl, whisk the egg whites until they are stiff. Pour the hot syrup over the whites, whisking constantly. Let cool.

4 Whisk the cream until it holds soft peaks. Add the Grand Marnier to the custard and fold this into the meringue, along with the cream. Pour into the prepared ramekins. Freeze overnight. Remove the paper collars. Let sit at room temperature for 30 minutes before serving.

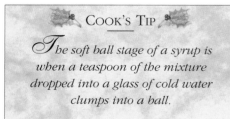

COOK'S TIP

The soft ball stage of a syrup is when a teaspoon of the mixture dropped into a glass of cold water clumps into a ball.

TIRAMISU IN CHOCOLATE CUPS

Give in to the temptation of tiramisù, with its magical mocha flavor.

INGREDIENTS

1 egg yolk
2 tablespoons superfine sugar
½ teaspoon vanilla extract
generous 1 cup mascarpone cheese
½ cup strong black coffee
1 tablespoon cocoa powder
2 tablespoons coffee liqueur
16 amaretti cookies
cocoa powder, for dusting

For the Chocolate Cups
6 ounces good quality bittersweet
chocolate, broken into squares
2 tablespoons unsalted butter

Serves 6

COOK'S TIP

When spreading the chocolate for the cups, don't aim for perfectly regular edges; uneven edges will give a prettier, frilled effect.

1 Make the chocolate cups. Cut out six 6-inch rounds of parchment paper. Melt the chocolate with the butter in a heatproof bowl over barely simmering water. Stir until smooth, then spread a spoonful of the chocolate mixture over each circle to within ¾ inch of the edge.

2 Carefully lift each paper round and drape it over an upturned teacup or ramekin so that the edges curve into frills. Let sit until completely set, then carefully peel off the paper to reveal the chocolate cups.

3 To make the filling, beat the egg yolk and sugar in a bowl until smooth, then stir in the vanilla extract and mascarpone. Mix until a smooth, creamy consistency is achieved.

4 In a separate bowl, mix the coffee, cocoa and liqueur. Break up the cookies and stir into the mixture.

5 Divide half the cookie mixture among the chocolate cups, then spoon on half the mascarpone mixture.

6 Spoon on the remaining cookie mixture, top with the rest of the mascarpone mixture and dust with cocoa. Serve as soon as possible.

ICED PRALINE TORTE

Make this elaborate torte several days ahead, decorate it and return it to the freezer until you are nearly ready to serve it. Let the torte stand at room temperature for an hour before serving, or leave it in the refrigerator overnight to soften.

INGREDIENTS

1 cup almonds or hazelnuts
½ cup superfine sugar
⅔ cup raisins
6 tablespoons rum or brandy
4 ounces bittersweet chocolate, broken into squares
2 tablespoons milk
2 cups heavy cream
2 tablespoons strong black coffee
16 ladyfinger cookies

To Finish
⅔ cup heavy cream
½ cup sliced almonds, toasted
½ ounce bittersweet chocolate, melted

Serves 8

1 To make the praline, have ready an oiled cake pan or baking sheet. Put the nuts in a heavy saucepan with the sugar and heat gently until the sugar melts. Swirl the pan to coat the nuts in the hot sugar. Cook slowly until the nuts brown and the sugar caramelizes. Watch constantly, as this will only take a few minutes. Transfer the nuts quickly into the cake pan or onto the baking sheet and let them cool completely. When cool, break the praline up and grind it to a fine powder in a food processor.

2 Soak the raisins in 3 tablespoons of the rum for an hour (or better still, overnight), so that they soften and absorb the full flavor of the alcohol. Melt the chocolate with the milk in a bowl over a pan of barely simmering water. Remove and let cool. Lightly grease a 6-cup loaf pan and line it with waxed paper.

3 Whisk the cream in a bowl until it holds soft peaks. Whisk in the cooled chocolate. Then fold in the praline and the soaked raisins, with any liquid.

4 Mix the coffee and remaining rum in a shallow dish. Dip in each of the ladyfinger cookies and arrange half in a layer over the bottom of the prepared loaf pan.

5 Cover the ladyfingers with the chocolate mixture and add another layer of soaked ladyfingers. Freeze overnight.

6 Dip the pan briefly into warm water to loosen it and transfer the torte to a serving plate. Cover with whipped cream. Sprinkle the top with toasted sliced almonds and drizzle the melted chocolate on top. Return the torte to the freezer until it is needed.

COOK'S TIP

Praline is a delicious crunchy caramel and nut mixture. It doesn't matter whether you use hazelnuts or almonds—or even a mixture of the two, if desired.

BAKED CUSTARDS WITH BURNT SUGAR

You can add a little liqueur to this dessert if desired, but it is equally delicious without it.

INGREDIENTS

2 vanilla pods
4 cups heavy cream
6 egg yolks
½ cup superfine sugar
2 tablespoons almond or orange liqueur
⅓ cup light brown sugar

Serves 6

> ### COOK'S TIP
> *To test whether the custards are ready, push the point of a knife into the center of one—if it comes out clean, the custards are done.*

1 Preheat the oven to 300°F. Place six ½-cup ramekins in a roasting pan or ovenproof dish and set aside.

2 With a sharp knife, split the vanilla pods lengthwise. Scrape the black seeds into a medium saucepan and add the pods. Add the cream and bring just to a boil over medium-high heat, stirring frequently. Remove from the heat and cover. Set aside for 15–20 minutes. This will let the vanilla infuse the cream.

3 In a bowl, whisk the egg yolks, superfine sugar and liqueur until well blended. Whisk in the hot cream and strain into a large bowl. Divide the custard equally among the ramekins.

4 Pour enough boiling water into the roasting pan to come halfway up the sides of the ramekins. Cover the pan with foil and bake for about 30 minutes, until the custards are just set. Remove the ramekins from the pan and let cool. Return to the dry roasting pan and let chill in the fridge for at least 2 hours or overnight.

5 Preheat the broiler. Sprinkle the sugar evenly over the surface of each custard and broil for 30–60 seconds, until the sugar melts and caramelizes. (Do not let the sugar burn or the custard curdle.) Place in the fridge again to set the crust and chill completely before serving.

CHRISTMAS CRANBERRY BOMBE

This is a light alternative for a Christmas dessert that is still very festive.

INGREDIENTS

For the Sorbet Center
2 cups fresh or frozen cranberries
⅔ cup orange juice
finely grated rind of ½ orange
½ teaspoon allspice
¼ cup sugar

For the Outer Layer
2⅔ cups vanilla ice cream
2 tablespoons chopped angelica
2 tablespoons candied citrus rind
1 tablespoon slivered almonds, toasted

Serves 6

3 Pack the mixture into a 6-cup mold and, using a metal spoon, hollow out the center. Freeze the mold until firm to the touch. This will take at least 3 hours.

4 Fill the hollowed-out center of the bombe with cranberry mixture, smooth over and freeze until firm. To serve, let soften slightly at room temperature, remove from the mold and slice.

1 Put the cranberries, orange juice, rind and spice in a pan and cook gently until the cranberries are soft. Add the sugar, then purée in a food processor until almost smooth, but still with some texture. Allow to cool.

2 Allow the vanilla ice cream to soften slightly, then stir in the chopped angelica, citrus rind and almonds.

183

CHOCOLATE SORBET WITH RED FRUITS

This velvety smooth sorbet has long been a favorite. Bittersweet chocolate gives by far the richest flavor, but if you don't have any on hand, then use nine ounces of the very best quality semisweet chocolate that you can find. If not, the sorbet will be too sweet.

INGREDIENTS

5 ounces bittersweet chocolate, roughly chopped
4 ounces semisweet chocolate, roughly chopped
1 cup superfine sugar
2 cups water
chocolate curls, to decorate
sprigs of fresh berries, to decorate

Serves 6

2 In a large heavy saucepan over medium-high heat, bring the sugar and water to a boil, stirring continuously, until the sugar dissolves. Boil for about 2 minutes, then remove the saucepan from the heat.

4 Strain the chocolate mixture into a large measuring cup or bowl and let cool, then chill, stirring occasionally. Freeze the mixture in an ice cream machine, following the manufacturer's instructions, or see Cook's Tip (below). Let the sorbet soften for 5–10 minutes at room temperature and serve in scoops, decorated with chocolate curls and sprigs of fresh berries.

1 Put the chopped bittersweet and semisweet chocolate in a food processor fitted with a metal blade and process for 20–30 seconds, until the chunks of chocolate are finely chopped.

3 With the food processor running, pour the hot syrup over the chocolate. Let the machine continue running for 1–2 minutes, until the chocolate is completely melted and the mixture is smooth, scraping down the bowl once.

COOK'S TIP

If you don't have an ice cream machine, freeze the sorbet until it is firm around the edges. Process the mixture until smooth, then freeze again.

AMARETTO MOUSSES WITH CHOCOLATE SAUCE

These little desserts are extremely rich and derive their flavor from amaretto, an

almond-flavored liqueur, and amaretti, little almond-flavored cookies.

INGREDIENTS

4 ounces amaretti, or macaroons
¼ cup Amaretto di Saronno liqueur
12 ounces white chocolate, broken into squares
1 envelope (½ ounce) powdered gelatin, soaked in 3 tablespoons cold water
2 cups heavy cream

For the Chocolate Sauce
8 ounces bittersweet chocolate, broken into squares
1¼ cups light cream or half-and-half
¼ cup superfine sugar

Serves 8

2 Melt the liqueur and white chocolate together in a bowl over a pan of hot but not boiling water. (Be very careful not to overheat the chocolate, or it will begin to separate and turn unpleasantly grainy.) Stir well until smooth; remove from the pan and let cool.

5 To make the chocolate sauce, put all the ingredients in a small saucepan and heat gently to melt the chocolate and dissolve the sugar. Simmer for 2–3 minutes. Let cool completely.

1 Lightly oil eight individual ½-cup molds and line the bottom of each mold with a small disk of oiled waxed paper. Put the cookies in a large bowl and crush them finely with a rolling pin.

3 Melt the gelatin over hot water and blend it into the chocolate mixture. Whisk the cream until it holds soft peaks. Gently fold in the chocolate mixture, with ¼ cup of the crushed cookies.

4 Put a teaspoonful of the crushed cookies in the bottom of each mold and spoon in the chocolate mixture. Tap each mold to disperse any air bubbles. Level the tops and sprinkle the remaining crushed cookies on top. Press down gently and chill for 4 hours.

6 Slip a knife around the sides of each mold, and turn out onto individual plates. Remove the waxed paper and pour a little dark chocolate sauce around each mousse.

COOK'S TIP

When melting chocolate, always set the bowl over a half-full pan of barely simmering water; chocolate reacts badly to splashes of water and overheating.

CHOCOLATE CRÊPES WITH PLUMS AND PORT

A good dinner party dessert, this dish can be made in advance and always looks impressive.

INGREDIENTS

*2 ounces bittersweet chocolate, broken
into squares
scant 1 cup milk
½ cup light cream or half-and-half
2 tablespoons cocoa powder
1 cup flour
2 eggs
oil, for frying*

*For the Filling
1¼ pounds red or golden plums
¼ cup superfine sugar
2 tablespoons water
2 tablespoons port
¾ cup crème fraîche*

*For the Sauce
5 ounces bittersweet chocolate, broken
into squares
¾ cup heavy cream
2 tablespoons port*

Serves 6

1 Place the chocolate in a saucepan with the milk. Heat gently until the chocolate has dissolved. Pour into a blender or food processor and add the cream, cocoa powder, flour and eggs. Process until smooth, then transfer into a bowl and chill for 30 minutes.

2 Meanwhile, make the filling. Halve and pit the plums. Place them in a saucepan and add the sugar and water. Bring to a boil, then cover and simmer for about 10 minutes. Stir in the port; simmer for another 30 seconds. Remove from the heat and keep warm.

3 Have ready a sheet of parchment paper. Heat a crêpe pan, grease it lightly with a little oil, then pour in just enough batter to cover the base of the pan, swirling to coat evenly. Cook until the crêpe has set, then flip it over to cook the other side. Slide the crêpe out onto the sheet of parchment, then cook 9–11 more crêpes in the same way.

4 Make the chocolate sauce. Combine the chocolate and cream in a saucepan. Heat gently, stirring until smooth. Add the port and heat gently for 1 minute.

5 Divide the plum filling among the crêpes, add a generous spoonful of crème fraîche to each and roll them up. Serve with the chocolate sauce.

CHOCOLATE, DATE AND ALMOND FILO COIL

Experience the allure of the Middle East with this delectable dessert. Crisp filo pastry conceals

a chocolate and rose water filling studded with dates and almonds.

INGREDIENTS

*1 package (10 ounces) filo pastry, thawed
if frozen
4 tablespoons (½ stick) unsalted butter,
melted
confectioners' sugar, cocoa powder and
ground cinnamon, for dusting*

For the Filling
*6 tablespoons unsalted butter
4 ounces bittersweet chocolate, broken
into squares
1 cup ground almonds
⅔ cup chopped dates
⅔ cup confectioners' sugar
2 teaspoons rosewater
½ teaspoon ground cinnamon*

Serves 6

1 Preheat the oven to 350°F. Grease an 8½-inch round cake pan. Make the chocolate, date and almond filling. Melt the butter with the chocolate in a heatproof bowl over a saucepan of barely simmering water, then remove the saucepan from the heat and stir in all of the remaining ingredients to make a thick paste. Set the pan aside to cool.

2 Lay one sheet of the filo pastry on a clean work surface. Brush the filo with melted butter, then lay a second sheet of filo on top and brush again with butter.

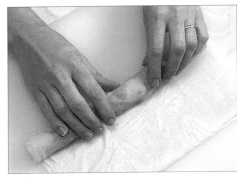

3 Roll a handful of the chocolate almond mixture into a long sausage shape and place along one edge of the filo. Roll into a tight coil.

4 Place the roll around the the pan. Make enough rolls to fill the pan.

5 Brush the coil with the melted butter. Bake for 30–35 minutes, until the pastry is golden brown and crisp. Remove the coil from the pan; place it on a plate. Serve warm, dusted with confectioners' sugar, cocoa and cinnamon.

189

RASPBERRY AND WHITE CHOCOLATE CHEESECAKE

Raspberries and white chocolate are an irresistible combination, especially when

teamed with smooth, rich mascarpone cheese on a crunchy ginger and pecan base.

INGREDIENTS

4 tablespoons (½ stick) unsalted butter
8 ounces ginger snaps, crushed
½ cup chopped pecans or walnuts

For the Filling
1¼ cups mascarpone cheese
¾ cup cream cheese
2 eggs, beaten
3 tablespoons superfine sugar
9 ounces white chocolate, broken into squares
1½ cups fresh or frozen raspberries

For the Topping
½ cup mascarpone cheese
⅓ cup cream cheese
white chocolate curls and raspberries, to decorate

Serves 8

2 To make the filling, beat the mascarpone cheese and cream cheese in a bowl, then beat in the eggs and superfine sugar until evenly mixed.

3 Melt the white chocolate gently in a heatproof bowl over hot water, then stir into the cheese mixture with the raspberries.

4 Transfer into the prepared pan and spread evenly, then bake for 1 hour, or until just set. Turn off the oven, but do not remove the cheesecake. Let sit until cool and completely set.

5 Remove the sides of the pan and carefully lift the cheesecake onto a serving plate. Make the topping by combining the mascarpone and cream cheese in a bowl and spreading the mixture over the cheesecake. Decorate with white chocolate curls and fresh raspberries.

COOK'S TIP

The cookies for the crust should be crushed quite finely. This can easily be done in a food processor. Alternatively, place the cookies in a sturdy plastic bag and crush them with a rolling pin.

1 Preheat the oven to 300°F. Melt the butter in a large saucepan, then stir in the crushed cookies and chopped nuts. Press the mixture into the bottom of a 9-inch springform cake pan.

CHOCOLATE ROULADE WITH COCONUT CREAM

This wonderfully rich roulade is the ultimate Christmas treat.

It also makes a perfect dessert for a New Year's Eve dinner party.

INGREDIENTS

¾ cup superfine sugar
5 eggs, separated
½ cup cocoa powder

For the Filling
1¼ cups heavy cream
3 tablespoons whiskey
1 piece (2 ounces) solid creamed
coconut
2 tablespoons superfine sugar

For the Topping
coarsely grated curls of fresh coconut
chocolate curls

Serves 8

1 Preheat the oven to 350°F. Grease and line a 13 x 9-inch jelly-roll pan. Dust a large sheet of waxed paper with 2 tablespoons of superfine sugar.

2 Place the egg yolks in a heatproof bowl. Add the remaining superfine sugar and whisk with a handheld electric mixer until the mixture is thick enough to leave a trail. Sift the cocoa on top, then fold in carefully and evenly with a metal spoon.

3 Whisk the egg whites in a clean, greasefree bowl until they form soft peaks. Fold about 1 tablespoon of the whites into the chocolate mixture to lighten it, then evenly fold in the rest.

4 Scrape the mixture into the prepared pan, pushing it right into the corners. Smooth the surface with a spatula, then bake for 20–25 minutes, or until well risen and springy to the touch.

5 Transfer the cooked sponge out onto the sugar-dusted waxed paper and carefully peel off the lining paper. Cover with a damp, clean dish towel and let cool.

COOK'S TIP

Either Irish or Scotch whiskey can be used to make the cream filling for this dessert. You can also use white rum or a rum-based spirit, such as Malibu, as an alternative.

6 To make the filling, whisk the cream with the whiskey in a bowl until the mixture just holds its shape, then finely grate the creamed coconut and stir it in with the sugar.

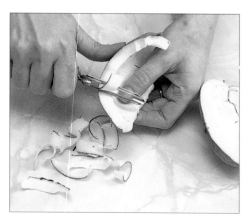

7 Remove the dish towel to uncover the sponge. Spread the sponge with about three-quarters of the cream mixture, right up to the edges. Roll up carefully from a long side. Transfer the roulade to a plate and pipe or spoon the remaining cream mixture on top. Then grate the fresh coconut to make the curls and place them on top along with the chocolate curls.

Christmas Baking

*N*uts and spices, dried fruit and mincemeat all
mean Christmas—and the delicious cakes and cookies baked
during this time. Some, such as the Moist and Rich Christmas
Cake, need advance preparation, while others, such as the
Christmas Cookies, are simple enough to make with
children. Gingerbread is essential to Christmas, and there are
recipes here that can be used to make pretty tree decorations and
a table centerpiece. There are the traditional Italian Panettone
and Austrian Stollen, New Year's Shortbread and Middle Eastern
Date-filled Pastries. Finally, there are three terrific recipes
with mincemeat—the all-time favorite—to ensure that
everyone finishes a festive meal feeling satisfied.

FESTIVE GINGERBREAD

In all its forms, gingerbread has been part of the Christmas tradition for generations.

It is particularly well-loved in Germany, from which many present-day baking traditions originate.

INGREDIENTS

2 tablespoons dark corn syrup
1 tablespoon molasses
¼ cup light brown sugar
2 tablespoons butter
1½ cups all-purpose flour
¾ teaspoon baking soda
½ teaspoon pumpkin pie spice
1½ teaspoons ground ginger
1 egg yolk

Icing and Decoration
½ quantity royal icing (see Introduction)
red, yellow and green food coloring
brightly colored ribbons

Makes 20

1 Preheat the oven to 375°F. Line several baking sheets with baking parchment. Place the corn syrup, molasses, sugar and butter in a saucepan. Heat gently, stirring occasionally, until the butter has melted into the syrup.

2 Sift the flour, baking soda, pumpkin pie spice and ginger together in a mixing bowl. Using a wooden spoon, stir in the molasses mixture and the egg yolk and mix to form a soft dough. Remove the dough from the bowl and knead on a lightly floured surface until smooth.

3 Roll out the dough thinly, and using a selection of festive cutters such as stars and Christmas trees, stamp out as many shapes as possible, kneading and rerolling the dough as necessary. Arrange the shapes, well spaced, on the baking sheets. Make a hole in the top of each shape, using a drinking straw, if you wish to use the cookies as hanging decorations.

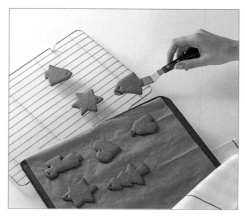

4 Bake for 15–20 minutes, or until risen and golden, and let cool on the baking sheets before transferring to a wire rack using a spatula.

5 Divide the royal icing into quarters and color one red, one yellow and one green. Make four waxed-paper piping bags and fill each one with a different-colored icing. Fold down the tops and snip off the points.

6 Pipe lines, dots, and zigzags on the gingerbread cookies using the icings. Let dry. If you intend to hang the cookies, thread ribbons through the holes made in the cookies.

COOK'S TIP

These brightly decorated gingerbread cookies are fun to make and may be used as edible Christmas-tree decorations.

GINGERBREAD HEART RING

This table centerpiece is inspired by traditional Polish Christmas decorations. You could make the

centerpiece with other cutout shapes, such as gingerbread men and women, teddy bears or stars.

EQUIPMENT

stiff cardboard
pencil and scissors
glaze made with 1 cup sifted
confectioners' sugar and, if desired,
colored red
spatula
7 heart-shaped gingerbread cookies,
baked and decorated
2-inch-wide ribbon
Victorian-style paper scraps (optional)

1 On a piece of stiff cardboard, draw a ring shape with an outer diameter of 10 inches and an inner diameter of 6 inches. Cut out the ring with a pair of scissors. Cover the cardboard ring with the glaze, using a spatula, and quickly—before it sets—press on the heart-shaped gingerbread cookies to cover it. Set the ring aside until the glaze has dried and the gingerbread cookies are firmly in place.

2 Tie the ribbon into a bow, trim the ends and attach it to the ring with a generous dab of glaze icing to ensure that it stays securely in place throughout the season. To preserve the ring as a decoration throughout the Christmas holidays, it may be wise to make extra heart-shaped cookies for young gingerbread enthusiasts to eat!

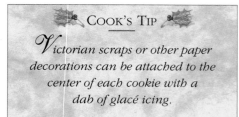

COOK'S TIP

Victorian scraps or other paper decorations can be attached to the center of each cookie with a dab of glacé icing.

GLAZE

Sift the required amount of confectioners' sugar into a bowl. Add a few drops of water at a time, and beat into the confectioners' sugar. Keep adding water until the desired consistency has been achieved.

Nut and Candied Fruit Ring

This cake can be made two or three weeks before Christmas. Store it in a tin in a cool place until needed.

INGREDIENTS

¼ cup rum, brandy or sherry
½ cup candied cherries, quartered
⅔ cup raisins
1 cup dried apricots, quartered
1 cup prunes, pitted and quartered
½ cup pitted and chopped dates
8 tablespoons (1 stick) butter
½ cup dark brown sugar
½ teaspoon ground cinnamon
½ teaspoon pumpkin pie spice
2 eggs, beaten
⅔ cup ground almonds
1 cup coarsely chopped walnuts
2 cups self-rising flour

To Finish
2 tablespoons rum, brandy or sherry
¼ cup apricot jam
whole blanched almonds, split
3 candied cherries, halved
a few strips of angelica

Makes 1 ring

1 The day before you want to bake the cake, put the rum in a large mixing bowl and add all the dried fruit. Cover the bowl with plastic wrap and let sit overnight in a cool place, so that the fruit is well soaked. Meanwhile, grease a 9-inch ring mold with a 6-cup capacity.

2 The next day, preheat the oven to 325°F. In a large mixing bowl, whisk the butter, sugar and spices together until they are light and fluffy. Whisk in the eggs, and then fold in the soaked fruits, with any of the remaining liquid. Mix the ground almonds and chopped walnuts into the bowl and sift in the flour.

3 Spoon the mixture into the prepared cake pan. Level the top of the mixture with the back of a spoon and bake in the preheated oven for 1½–2 hours. Leave the cake to cool in the pan for 30 minutes, then turn out onto a wire rack and allow to cool completely. Brush the cake with the finishing rum, brandy or sherry.

4 Make a glaze by heating the apricot jam in a small pan to melt it; then brush the top of the cake with hot glaze; arrange the nuts and fruit in a flower design on top and brush them liberally with more apricot glaze. The glaze must be very hot, or the decoration will lift while you are brushing it.

199

PANETTONE

This popular Italian cake is perfect for the festive season.

INGREDIENTS

⅔ cup lukewarm milk
1 package active dry yeast
3–3½ cups flour
⅓ cup sugar
2 teaspoons salt
2 eggs
5 egg yolks
12 tablespoons (1½ sticks) unsalted butter,
at room temperature
¾ cup raisins
grated rind of 1 lemon
½ cup candied citrus peel, chopped

Makes 1 loaf

1 Combine the milk and yeast in a large, warmed mixing bowl and let sit for 10 minutes to dissolve the yeast.

2 Sift in 1 cup of the flour, cover loosely, and let sit in a warm place for 30 minutes.

3 Sift in the remaining flour. Make a well in the center and add the sugar, salt, eggs and egg yolks.

4 Stir the dough mixture with a wooden spoon until it becomes too stiff, then continue to work the mixture with your hands to obtain a very elastic and sticky dough. Add a little more of the flour, if necessary, blending it in well, to keep the dough as soft as possible.

5 Smear the butter into the dough, then work it in with your hands. When evenly distributed, cover the dough and let rise in a warm place until doubled in volume, 3–4 hours.

6 Line the bottom of a 8-cup charlotte mold or 2-pound coffee can with waxed paper, then grease the bottom and sides.

7 Punch down the dough and transfer to a floured surface. Knead in the raisins, lemon rind, and citrus peel.

8 Transfer the dough to the mold. Cover with a plastic bag and let rise until the dough is well above the top of the container, about 2 hours.

9 Preheat the oven to 400°F. Bake for 15 minutes, cover with foil, and lower the heat to 350°F. Bake for 30 minutes. Cool in the mold, then unmold the cake on a rack.

STOLLEN

Stollen is a fruity yeast bread traditionally served in Austria and Germany at

Christmastime. It may be served at breakfast with coffee or tea.

INGREDIENTS

⅔ cup lukewarm milk
3 tablespoons superfine sugar
1 package (2 teaspoons) active dry yeast
3 cups all-purpose flour, plus extra for dusting
¼ teaspoon salt
8 tablespoons (1 stick) butter, softened
1 egg, beaten
⅓ cup raisins
⅓ cup golden raisins
⅓ cup candied orange peel, chopped
½ cup blanched almonds, chopped
1 tablespoon rum
3 tablespoons butter, melted
about ½ cup confectioners' sugar

Makes 1 loaf

1 Combine the warm milk, sugar and yeast and let sit in a warm place until it is frothy.

2 Sift together the flour and salt, make a well in the center and pour in the yeast mixture. Add the softened butter and egg and mix to form a soft dough. Mix in the raisins, golden raisins, orange peel and almonds and sprinkle the rum. Knead the dough on a lightly floured board until it is pliable.

3 Place the dough in a large, greased mixing bowl, cover it with baking parchment and set aside in a warm place for about 2 hours, until it has doubled in size.

4 Transfer the dough to a floured board and knead it lightly until it is smooth and elastic again. Shape the dough to a rectangle, about 10 x 8 inches. Fold the dough over along one of the long sides and press the 2 layers together. Cover the loaf and let it stand for 20 minutes.

5 Heat the oven to 400°F. Bake the loaf on a baking sheet for 25–30 minutes, or until it is well risen. Let it cool slightly on the baking sheet, then brush it with melted butter. Sift the sugar over the top and transfer the loaf to a wire rack to cool. Serve the stollen in thin slices.

LIGHT JEWELED FRUIT CAKE

This cake can be made up to two weeks before eating it. For serving, brush the top

with hot apricot jam and tie a pretty ribbon around the sides.

INGREDIENTS

½ cup currants
⅔ cup golden raisins
1 cup quartered candied cherries
½ cup finely chopped candied citrus peel
2 tablespoons rum, brandy or sherry
1 cup butter
1 cup superfine sugar
finely grated rind of 1 orange
finely grated rind of 1 lemon
4 eggs
½ cup chopped almonds
⅔ cup ground almonds
2 cups flour

To Finish
1 cup whole blanched almonds

Makes 1 cake

1 The day before you want to bake the cake, soak the currants, raisins, candied cherries and citrus peel in the rum. Cover with plastic wrap and let sit overnight. The next day, grease and line an 8-inch round cake pan or a 7-inch square cake pan with a double thickness of waxed paper.

2 Preheat the oven to 325°F. In a large bowl, whisk the butter, sugar and orange and lemon rinds together until they are light and fluffy. Beat in the eggs, one at a time.

3 Mix in the chopped almonds, ground almonds, soaked fruits (with their liquid) and the flour, to make a batter with a soft, dropping consistency. Spoon into the cake pan. Bake for 30 minutes.

4 Gently place the whole almonds in a pattern on top of the cake. Do not press them into the cake, or they will sink during cooking. Return the cake to the oven and cook for another 1½–2 hours, or until the center is firm to the touch. Let the cake cool in the pan for 30 minutes. Then remove it and cool completely on a wire rack, but leave the paper on; this helps to keep the cake moist while stored.

SPICED CHRISTMAS CAKE

This light cake mixture is flavored with spices and fruit. It can be served with

a dusting of confectioners' sugar and decorated with holly leaves.

INGREDIENTS

½ pound (2 sticks) butter, plus extra for greasing
1 tablespoon fresh white bread crumbs
1 cup superfine sugar
¼ cup water
3 eggs, separated
2 cups self-rising flour
1½ teaspoons pumpkin pie spice
2 tablespoons chopped angelica
2 tablespoons mixed citrus peel
¼ cup chopped candied cherries
½ cup chopped walnuts
confectioners' sugar, to dust

Makes 1 cake

1 Preheat the oven to 350°F. Brush a 6-cup fluted ring mold with a little melted butter and coat with bread crumbs, shaking out any excess.

2 Place the butter, sugar and water in a saucepan. Heat gently, stirring occasionally, until melted. Boil for 3 minutes, until syrupy, then let cool. Place the egg whites in a clean bowl and whisk until stiff. Sift the flour and spice into a bowl, add the angelica, citrus peel, cherries and walnuts and stir well to mix. Add the egg yolks.

3 Pour the cooled butter mixture into the bowl and beat to form a soft batter. Gradually fold in the egg whites, until the mixture is evenly blended. Pour into the prepared mold and bake for 50–60 minutes or until the cake springs back when pressed in the center. Remove from the pan and let cool on a wire rack. Dust with confectioners' sugar to serve.

MOIST AND RICH CHRISTMAS CAKE

This cake can be made four to six weeks before Christmas. During this time, pierce the cake periodically

with a fine needle and spoon on two to three tablespoons brandy.

INGREDIENTS

1⅓ cups golden raisins
1 cup currants
1⅓ cups raisins
1 cup pitted, chopped prunes
¼ cup halved candied cherries
⅓ cup chopped mixed citrus peel
3 tablespoons brandy or sherry
2 cups flour
pinch of salt
½ teaspoon ground cinnamon
½ teaspoon grated nutmeg
1 tablespoon cocoa powder
½ pound (2 sticks) butter
1 generous cup dark brown sugar
4 large eggs
finely grated rind of 1 orange or lemon
⅔ cup ground almonds
½ cup chopped almonds

To Decorate
(see Introduction)
¼ cup apricot jam
1 pound almond paste
1 pound fondant icing
8 ounces royal icing

Makes 1 cake

1 The day before you want to bake the cake, soak the dried fruit in the brandy, cover and let sit overnight. The next day, grease an 8-inch round cake pan and line it with waxed paper.

2 Preheat the oven to 325°F. Sift together the flour, salt, spices and cocoa powder. In a separate bowl, whisk the butter and sugar together until light and fluffy, then gradually beat in the eggs. Mix in the orange or lemon rind, ground and chopped almonds, dried fruits (with any liquid) and flour mixture.

3 Spoon into the cake pan, level the top and give the cake pan a gentle tap on the work surface to disperse any air bubbles. Bake for 3 hours, or until a fine skewer inserted into the middle comes out clean. Transfer the cake pan to a wire rack and let the cake cool in the pan for an hour. Then invert the cake from the pan, onto the wire rack, but leave the paper on, as it will help to keep the cake moist during storage. When the cake has cooled, wrap it in foil and store it in a cool place.

4 Warm the apricot jam, then sieve it to make a glaze. Remove the paper from the cake, place it in the center of a cake board and brush it with hot apricot glaze. Cover the cake with a layer of almond paste and then a layer of fondant icing. Pipe a border around the base of the cake with royal icing. Tie a ribbon around the sides.

5 Roll out any trimmings from the fondant icing and stamp out 12 small holly leaves with a cutter. Make one bell motif with a cookie cutter, dusted first with sifted confectioners' sugar. Roll 36 small balls for the holly berries. Let the decorations dry for 24 hours on waxed paper to. Decorate the cake with the fondant icing leaves, berries and bell, attaching them to the cake with a dab of royal icing. Let the icing dry, then cover the cake and pack in an airtight tin until needed.

ORANGE SHORTBREAD FINGERS

These are a real teatime treat. The fingers will keep in an airtight tin for up to two weeks.

INGREDIENTS

8 tablespoons (1 stick) unsalted butter
¼ cup superfine sugar, plus a little extra
for sprinkling
finely grated rind of 2 oranges
1½ cups flour

Makes 18

COOK'S TIP

This recipe is a lifesaver for busy cooks. It is a good idea to make extra dough and store it, well wrapped, in the freezer. When guests arrive unexpectedly, you will be able to make up freshly baked shortbread fingers in minutes.

1 Preheat the oven to 375°F. Beat the butter and sugar together until they are soft and creamy. Beat in the orange rind. Gradually add the flour and gently pull the dough together to form a soft ball.

2 Roll the dough out on a lightly floured surface until about ½ inch thick. Cut it into fingers, sprinkle on a little extra sugar, prick with a fork and bake for about 20 minutes or until the fingers are a light golden color.

New Year's Shortbread

Light, crisp shortbread looks very professional when shaped in a mold,

although you could also shape it by hand.

INGREDIENTS

¾ *cup flour*

¼ *cup cornstarch*

¼ *cup superfine sugar*

8 tablespoons (1 stick) unsalted butter

Makes 2 large or 8 individual
shortbreads

COOK'S TIP

*The secret of successful
shortbread baking is to have cool
hands when working the butter and
sugar together.*

1 Preheat the oven to 325°F. Lightly flour the mold and line a baking sheet with parchment paper. Sift the flour, cornstarch and sugar into a large mixing bowl. Cut the butter into pieces and rub into the flour mixture, using your fingertips or a food processor. When the mixture begins to bind together, you can knead it into a soft dough, using your hands.

2 Place the dough in the mold and press to fit neatly. Invert the mold onto the baking sheet and tap firmly to release the dough shape. Bake for about 35–40 minutes or until the shortbread is pale golden in color.

3 Sprinkle the top of the shortbread with a little superfine sugar and set aside to cool on the baking sheet. Wrap the shortbread in cellophane and pack in an airtight tin, or place in a box tied with ribbons, to give as a gift.

CHRISTMAS COOKIES

These cookies are great fun for children to make as presents. Any shape of cookie cutters can be used.

Store the cookies in an airtight tin, and for a change, omit the lemon rind and add ⅓ cup

of ground almonds and a few drops of almond extract.

INGREDIENTS

6 tablespoons (¾ stick) butter
generous ½ cup confectioners' sugar
finely grated rind of 1 small lemon
1 egg yolk
1½ cups flour
pinch of salt

To Decorate
2 egg yolks
red and green edible food coloring

Makes about 12

1 In a large bowl, beat the butter, sugar and lemon rind together until pale and fluffy. Beat in the egg yolk and then sift in the flour and the salt. Knead to form a smooth dough. Wrap in plastic wrap and chill for 30 minutes.

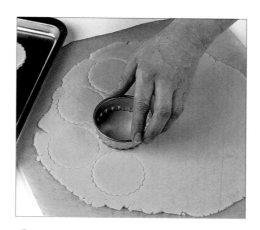

2 Preheat the oven to 375°F. On a lightly floured surface, roll out the dough to ⅛ inch thick. Using a 2½-inch fluted cutter, stamp out as many cookies as you can, with the cutter dipped in flour to prevent it from sticking to the dough.

3 Transfer the cookies to lightly greased baking sheets. Mark the tops lightly with a 1-inch holly-leaf cutter and use a ¼-inch plain piping nozzle for the berries. Chill for 10 minutes, or until firm.

4 Meanwhile, put each egg yolk into a small cup. Mix red food coloring into one and green food coloring into the other. Using a small, clean paintbrush, carefully paint the colors onto the cookies. Bake the cookies for 10–12 minutes, or until they begin to color around the edges. Let them cool slightly on the baking sheets, and then transfer them to a wire rack to cool completely.

COOK'S TIP

When cooking with young children, things will flow more smoothly if you have all the ingredients prepared before they start to cook. It is a good idea to provide large aprons for all involved!

GINGER FLORENTINES

These colorful, chewy cookies are delicious served with ice cream and are certain to disappear

as soon as they are served. Store them in an airtight container.

INGREDIENTS

4 tablespoons (½ stick) butter
½ cup superfine sugar
¼ cup chopped mixed candied cherries
2 tablespoons chopped orange peel
½ cup sliced almonds
½ cup chopped walnuts
1 tablespoon chopped candied ginger
2 tablespoons flour
½ teaspoon ground ginger

To Finish
2 ounces bittersweet chocolate
2 ounces white chocolate

Makes 30

1 Preheat the oven to 350°F. Whisk together the butter and sugar in a mixing bowl until they are light and fluffy. Thoroughly mix in all the remaining ingredients, except for the chocolate.

2 Cut a piece of baking parchment large enough to fit your baking sheets. Put 4 small spoonfuls of the mixture on each tray, spacing them well apart to allow for spreading. Gently flatten the cookies with the palm of your hand and bake them in the preheated oven for 5 minutes.

3 Remove the cookies from the oven and flatten them with a wet fork, shaping them into neat rounds. Return to the oven for 3–4 minutes, until they are golden brown.

4 Let the cookies cool on the baking sheets for 2 minutes to firm up and then, using a spatula, carefully transfer them to a wire rack. When the cookies are cool and firm, melt the bittersweet and the white chocolate. Spread dark chocolate on the undersides of half the cookies and spread white chocolate on the undersides of the rest.

CHOCOLATE KISSES

These rich little cookies look attractive arranged on a plate and dusted with confectioners' sugar.

Serve them with ice cream or simply as a sweet accompaniment to coffee.

INGREDIENTS

3 ounces bittersweet chocolate, broken into squares
3 ounces white chocolate, broken into squares
8 tablespoons (1 stick) butter
½ cup superfine sugar
2 eggs
2 cups flour
confectioners' sugar, to decorate

Makes 24

3 Halve the mixture and divide it between the two bowls of melted chocolate. Mix the chocolate into the dough mixture thoroughly. Knead the doughs until smooth and pliable, wrap them in plastic wrap and set aside to chill for about 1 hour. Preheat the oven to 375°F.

4 Shape slightly rounded teaspoonfuls of both doughs roughly into balls. Roll the balls in the palms of your hands to make neater ball shapes. Arrange the balls on greased baking trays and bake them for 10–12 minutes. Dust with sifted confectioners' sugar and then transfer them to a wire rack to cool.

1 Put the dark and white chocolate into each of two bowls and melt each one over a pan of hot water. Set aside.

2 Whisk together the butter and superfine sugar until they are pale and fluffy. Gradually beat in the eggs, one at a time. Sift in the flour and mix together well.

DATE-FILLED PASTRIES

The secret of these pastries is to get as much date filling into the pastry as possible,

but you must make sure to seal the opening well.

INGREDIENTS

6 tablespoons margarine or butter,
softened
1½ cups flour
1 teaspoon rosewater
1 teaspoon orange flower water
3 tablespoons water
2 tablespoons sifted confectioners' sugar
for sprinkling

For the Filling
⅔ cup pitted dried dates
¼ cup boiling water
½ teaspoon orange flower water

Makes about 25

1 To make the filling, chop the dates finely. Add ¼ cup boiling water and the orange flower water, beat the mixture and let cool.

2 To make the pastries, rub the shortening into the flour. Add the flower waters and the water and mix.

3 Once the dough feels firm, shape it into about 25 small balls.

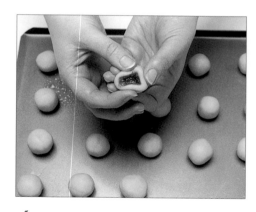

4 Preheat the oven to 350°F. Press your finger into each ball to make a small hollow, pressing the sides over and over to make the walls thinner. Put about ¼ teaspoon of the date mixture into each one and seal by pressing the pastry together.

5 Arrange the date pastries, seam side down, on a lightly greased baking sheet and prick each one with a fork. Bake for 15–20 minutes, then transfer to a wire rack and let cool completely.

6 Put the pastries on a plate and lightly sprinkle the sifted confectioners' sugar over them. Shake gently to make sure they are well covered. Date-filled pastries will freeze very well until needed.

Cinnamon Rolls

These pretty little pastry whirls, scented with cinnamon, are sure to be coffee-time favorites.

INGREDIENTS

For the Dough
1⅔ cups flour
½ teaspoon salt
2 tablespoons sugar
1 envelope (1 teaspoon) active dry yeast
3 tablespoons vegetable oil
1 egg
½ cup warm milk
½ cup warm water

For the Filling
2 tablespoons butter, softened
½ cup dark brown sugar
½–1 teaspoon ground cinnamon
1 tablespoon raisins

Makes 24 small rolls

1 Sift the flour into a large mixing bowl, then add the salt and sugar and sprinkle on the yeast. Combine the oil, egg, milk and water and add to the flour. Mix to a dough, then knead until smooth. Let the dough rise until it has doubled in size and then knock it back again.

2 Roll out the dough into a large rectangle and cut in half vertically. Spread with the soft butter, reserving 1 tablespoon for brushing. Mix the sugar and cinnamon and sprinkle over the top. Dot with the raisins. Roll each piece of dough into a long jellyroll shape to enclose the filling.

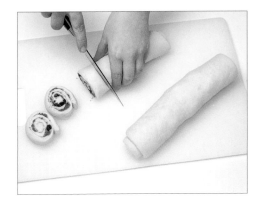

3 Cut each piece into 1-inch slices and arrange on a baking sheet. Brush with butter. Let rise for 30 minutes.

4 Preheat the oven to 400°F. Bake the rolls for 20 minutes. Let cool on a wire rack.

AMARETTI

If bitter almonds are not available, substitute with regular almonds.

INGREDIENTS

1¼ cups sweet almonds
½ cup bitter almonds
1 cup superfine sugar
2 egg whites
½ teaspoon almond extract
1 teaspoon vanilla extract
confectioners' sugar, for dusting

Makes about 36

1 Preheat the oven to 325°F. Peel the almonds by dropping them into a pan of boiling water for 1–2 minutes. Drain. Rub off the skins.

2 Place the almonds on a baking sheet and let them dry out in the oven for 10–15 minutes without browning.

3 Grind the almonds with half the sugar in a food processor. Beat the egg whites until they hold soft peaks. Sprinkle on half the remaining sugar and continue beating until stiff peaks form. Fold in the remaining sugar, the extracts and ground almonds.

4 Spoon the almond mixture into a pastry bag with a smooth nozzle. Line a flat baking sheet with baking parchment. Dust this with flour.

5 Pipe out the mixture in rounds the size of walnuts. Sprinkle lightly with the confectioners' sugar and let stand for 2 hours. Near the end of this time, turn the oven on again and

6 Bake the amaretti for 15 minutes or until they turn pale gold. Remove from the oven and let them cool on a rack. When completely cool, the cookies may be stored in an airtight container.

COOK'S TIP

*B*itter almonds can usually be found at good Italian delicatessens or health-food stores.

Mocha Viennese Swirls

Some temptations just can't be resisted.

Put out a plate of these "melt-in-your-mouth" marvels and watch them vanish.

INGREDIENTS

*4 ounces bittersweet chocolate, broken
into squares*
½ pound (2 sticks) unsalted butter
6 tablespoons confectioners' sugar
2 tablespoons strong black coffee
1¾ cups flour
½ cup cornstarch

To Decorate
about 20 blanched almonds
5 ounces bittersweet chocolate

Makes about 20

3 Spoon the batter into a piping bag fitted with a large star nozzle and pipe about 20 swirls onto the baking sheets.

4 Press an almond into the center of each of the swirls. Bake for about 15 minutes, or until the cookies are firm and just beginning to brown.

5 Let the cookies cool for about 10 minutes on the baking sheets, then lift them carefully onto a wire rack and let them cool completely.

6 When the cookies have cooled, melt the chocolate and dip the bottom of each swirl to coat. Place the coated cookies on a sheet of baking parchment and let set.

COOK'S TIP

If the mixture is too stiff to pipe, soften it by adding more black coffee, a little bit at a time.

1 Preheat the oven to 375°F. Lightly grease two large baking sheets. Melt the chocolate squares in a mixing bowl over hot water. Cream the butter with the confectioners' sugar in a bowl until smooth and pale. Beat in the melted chocolate, then the strong black coffee.

2 Sift the flour and cornstarch over the mixture in the bowl. Fold in lightly and evenly to make a soft batter.

DOUBLE-CRUST Mince Pies

Mince pies are an essential part of the culinary tradition and the Christmas season would not be complete without them. This recipe has an extra-special pastry shell for maximum delight.

INGREDIENTS

*shortcrust pastry made with
3 cups flour
butter, for greasing
flour for dusting
2 cups mincemeat
milk, for brushing
confectioners' sugar, for dusting*

Makes 24 pies

1 Preheat the oven to 400°F. Use a rolling pin to roll out the shortcrust pastry as thinly as possible on a lightly floured board. With a 3-inch plain round cutter, cut out 24 circles. With a 2-inch plain round cutter, cut out another 24 circles. Carefully lay the circles aside.

2 Grease a muffin pan with 24 mini cups, dust the cups with flour and line them with the larger pastry circles. Fill each one with mincemeat, then brush the edges with milk. Press the smaller rounds on top, seal the edges and brush tops with milk.

3 Bake for 25–30 minutes, until the pastry is light golden brown. Cool in the pan, then transfer the pies to a wire rack to cool. Store them in an airtight container. Just before serving, dust the tops with sugar. Serve the pies warm.

> ### COOK'S TIP
>
> *Today's mincemeat no longer contains meat or poultry as it once did, except in the form of suet. If you do not wish to eat animal fats, look for a mincemeat made with vegetarian suet.*

Almond Mincemeat Tartlets

Serve these little tartlets warm with brandy- or rum-flavored custard.

INGREDIENTS

2½ cups all-purpose flour
generous ¾ cup confectioners' sugar
1 teaspoon ground cinnamon
12 tablespoons (1½ sticks) butter
⅔ cup ground almonds
1 egg yolk
3 tablespoons milk
1 jar (1 pound) mincemeat
1 tablespoon brandy or rum

For the Lemon Sponge Filling
8 tablespoons (1 stick) butter or margarine
½ cup superfine sugar
1½ cups self-rising flour
2 large eggs
finely grated rind of 1 large lemon

For the Lemon Icing
1 generous cup confectioners' sugar
1 tablespoon lemon juice

Makes 36

3 For the lemon sponge filling, whisk the butter, sugar, flour, eggs and lemon rind together until smooth. Spoon on top of the mincemeat in the tartlet pans, dividing it evenly, and level the tops. Bake for 20–30 minutes, or until golden brown and springy to the touch. Remove and let cool on a wire rack.

4 For the lemon icing, sift the confectioners' sugar into a bowl and mix with the lemon juice to form a smooth, thick icing of coating consistency. Spoon into a piping bag and drizzle a zigzag pattern over each of the tartlets. If you're short on time, simply dust the tartlets with sifted confectioners' sugar before serving.

1 For the pastry, sift the flour, confectioners' sugar and cinnamon into a bowl and rub in the butter until the mixture resembles fine bread crumbs. Add the almonds and bind with the egg yolk and milk into a dough. Knead the dough until smooth, chill for 30 minutes.

2 Preheat the oven to 375°F. On a lightly floured surface, roll out the pastry and cut out 36 fluted rounds with a cookie cutter; use to line the tartlet pans. Mix the mincemeat with the brandy and put a teaspoonful in each pastry shell. Chill in the fridge.

Deluxe Mincemeat Tart

The mincemeat can be made and kept in the fridge for up to two weeks.

It can also be used to make individual mince pies.

INGREDIENTS

2 cups flour
2 teaspoons ground cinnamon
⅔ cup finely ground walnuts
8 tablespoons (1 stick) butter
¼ cup superfine sugar, plus extra
for dusting
1 egg
2 drops vanilla extract
1 tablespoon cold water

For the Mincemeat
2 apples, peeled, cored and
coarsely grated
1⅓ cups raisins
¾ cup dried apricots, chopped
¾ cup dried figs or prunes, chopped
1 small bunch green grapes, halved
and seeded
½ cup chopped almonds
finely grated rind of 1 lemon
2 tablespoons lemon juice
2 tablespoons brandy or port
¼ teaspoon pumpkin pie spice
generous ½ cup light brown sugar
2 tablespoons butter, melted

Serves 8

1 To make the pastry, put the flour, cinnamon and walnuts in a food processor. Add the butter and process until the mixture resembles fine bread crumbs. Transfer into a bowl and stir in the sugar. Using a fork, beat the egg with the vanilla extract and water. Gradually stir the egg mixture into the dry ingredients. Gather together with your fingertips to form a soft, pliable dough. Knead briefly on a lightly floured surface until smooth. Then wrap the dough in plastic wrap and chill in the fridge for 30 minutes.

2 Combine all of the mincemeat ingredients in a large bowl.

3 Cut off one-third of the pastry and reserve it for the lattice. Roll out the remainder and use it to line a 9-inch springform pan. Make a ¼-inch rim around the top edge.

4 With a rolling pin, roll off the excess pastry. Fill the shell with mincemeat.

5 Roll out the remaining pastry and cut it into ½-inch strips. Arrange the strips in a lattice over the top of the pastry, wet the seams and press them together well. Chill for 30 minutes.

6 Preheat the oven to 375°F. Place a baking sheet in the oven to preheat. Brush the pastry with water and dust it with superfine sugar. Bake the tart on the baking sheet for 30–40 minutes. Transfer to a wire rack and let cool for 15 minutes, then carefully remove the pan. Serve warm or cold, with sweetened whipped cream.

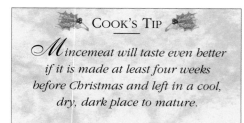

COOK'S TIP

Mincemeat will taste even better if it is made at least four weeks before Christmas and left in a cool, dry, dark place to mature.

Christmas Treats & Edible Gifts

There's nothing nicer to receive at Christmastime than a selection of homemade candies and treats in beautiful festive wrappings. If you're used to store-bought fudge or Turkish delight, you'll be astounded by the taste of these homemade versions. The same goes for the marshmallow recipe included here, which produces little pillows of mouthwatering delight. Though Marzipan Fruits and Fruit Fondant Chocolates take a little time and effort, the results will be well worth the trouble. Collections of cookies and individual cakes are a favorite Christmas treat, as are the Mini Black Buns, hiding their luscious filling inside. Try Flavored Vinegars and Fruits in Liqueurs for special gifts that taste as good as they look.

Creamy Fudge

A good selection of fudge always makes a welcome change from chocolates.

Mix and match the flavors to make a gift-wrapped assortment.

INGREDIENTS

*4 tablespoons (½ stick) unsalted butter,
plus extra for greasing
2 cups granulated sugar
1¼ cups heavy cream
⅔ cup milk
3 tablespoons water (this can be replaced
with orange, apricot or cherry brandy,
or strong coffee)*

Flavorings
*1 cup semisweet or milk
chocolate chips
1 cup chopped almonds, hazelnuts,
walnuts or brazil nuts
½ cup chopped candied cherries, dates or
dried apricots*

Makes 2 pounds

1 Grease an 8-inch shallow square pan. Place the butter, sugar, cream, milk and water or other flavorings in a large heavy saucepan. Heat very gently, until all the sugar has dissolved.

2 Bring the mixture to a rolling boil; boil until fudge reaches the soft stage.

3 If you are making chocolate-flavored fudge, add the chocolate chips to the mixture at this stage. Remove the saucepan from the heat and beat thoroughly until the mixture starts to thicken and become opaque.

4 Just before this consistency has been reached, add chopped nuts for a nutty fudge, or candied cherries or dried fruit for a fruit-flavored fudge. Beat well until evenly blended.

5 Pour the fudge into the prepared pan, taking care, as the mixture is very hot. Let the mixture sit until cool and almost set. Using a sharp knife, mark the fudge into small squares and let sit in the pan until quite firm.

6 Turn the fudge out onto a board and invert. Using a long-bladed knife, cut into squares. You can dust some squares with confectioners' sugar and drizzle others with melted chocolate, if desired.

ORANGE, MINT AND COFFEE MERINGUES

These tiny, crisp meringues are flavored with orange, coffee and mint chocolate sticks and liqueurs.

Pile them into dry, airtight glass jars or decorative tins.

INGREDIENTS

8 chocolate mint sticks
8 chocolate orange sticks
8 chocolate coffee sticks
½ teaspoon crème de menthe
½ teaspoon orange curaçao or Cointreau
½ teaspoon Tia Maria
3 egg whites
¾ cup superfine sugar
1 teaspoon cocoa

Makes 90

2 Place the egg whites in a clean bowl and whisk until stiff. Gradually add the sugar, whisking well after each addition, until thick. Add a third of the meringue to each bowl and fold in gently, using a clean spatula, until evenly blended.

3 Place about 30 teaspoons of each mixture on the baking sheets, spaced apart. Sprinkle the top of each meringue with the reserved chopped chocolate sticks. Bake for 1 hour or until crisp. Let cool, then dust with cocoa.

COOK'S TIP

These little meringues are ideal served with coffee after dinner. Alternatively, they make an original topping for ice-cream sundaes.

1 Preheat the oven to 225°F. Line two or three baking sheets with baking parchment. Chop each flavor of chocolate stick separately and place each into separate bowls, retaining a teaspoonful of each flavor of stick. Stir in the liquid flavorings to match the flavor of the chocolate sticks in the bowls.

Turkish Delight

Turkish Delight is always a favorite at Christmas, and this versatile recipe can be made in minutes. Try

different flavors such as lemon, crème de menthe and orange, and vary the colors accordingly.

INGREDIENTS

2 cups granulated sugar
1¼ cups water
1 envelope (2 tablespoons) powdered
gelatin
½ teaspoon tartaric acid
2 tablespoons rose water
pink food coloring
3 tablespoons confectioners' sugar, sifted
1 tablespoon cornstarch

Makes 1 pound

1 Wet the insides of two 7-inch shallow square pans with water. Place the sugar and 1 cup water in a heavy saucepan. Heat gently, stirring occasionally, until the sugar has dissolved.

2 Blend the gelatin and remaining ¼ cup water in a small bowl and place over a saucepan of hot water. Stir occasionally until dissolved. Bring the sugar syrup to a boil and boil steadily for about 8 minutes, or until the syrup registers 260°F on a candy thermometer. Stir the tartaric acid into the gelatin, then pour into the boiling syrup and stir until well blended. Remove from the heat.

3 Add the rose water and a few drops of pink food coloring and stir, adding a few more drops as necessary to tint the mixture pale pink. Pour the mixture into the prepared pans and let set for several hours or overnight. Dust a sheet of waxed paper with some of the confectioners' sugar and the cornstarch. Dip the bottom of the pans in hot water and invert them onto the paper. Cut the Turkish delight into 1-inch squares, using an oiled knife. Toss the squares in confectioners' sugar to coat evenly.

CANDIED FRUITS

These luxurious candies are very popular at Christmas, and they cost a fraction of the store price if made at home. The preparation is done over about four weeks, but the result is well worth the effort. Choose one type of fruit, or select a variety of fruits such as cherries, plums, peaches, apricots, starfruit, pineapple, apples, oranges, lemons, limes and clementines.

INGREDIENTS

1 pound fruit
4½ cups granulated sugar
1 cup powdered glucose

Makes 24 pieces

1 Pit cherries, plums, peaches and apricots. Peel and core pineapple and cut into cubes or rings. Peel, core and quarter apples and thinly slice citrus fruits. Prick cherry skins with a toothpick to extract the maximum flavor.

2 Place enough prepared fruit in a saucepan to cover the bottom, keeping individual fruit types together. Add water to cover the fruit and simmer gently, to avoid breaking it, until almost tender. Use a slotted spoon to transfer the fruit to a shallow dish, removing any skins if necessary. Repeat as above until all the fruit has been cooked.

3 Measure 1¼ cups of the cooking liquid, or make up this quantity with water if necessary. Pour into the clean saucepan and add ¼ cup sugar and the glucose. Heat gently, stirring occasionally, until dissolved. Bring to a boil and pour over the fruit in the dish, completely immersing it, and let sit overnight.

4 DAY 2. Drain the syrup into the pan and add ¼ cup sugar. Dissolve the sugar and bring to a boil. Pour over the fruit and let sit overnight. Repeat this process each day, draining off the syrup, dissolving ¼ cup sugar, boiling the syrup and immersing the fruit. Let sit overnight on Days 3, 4, 5, 6 and 7.

5 DAY 8. Drain the fruit, dissolve ½ cup sugar in the syrup and bring to a boil. Add the fruit and cook gently for 3 minutes. Return to the dish and let sit for 2 days. DAY 10. Repeat as for Day 8. The syrup should now look like honey. Let sit in the dish for at least 10 days, or up to 3 weeks.

6 Place a wire rack over a baking sheet. Remove each piece of fruit with a slotted spoon, and arrange on the rack. Dry the fruit in a warm, dry place or in the oven at the lowest setting until the surface no longer feels sticky. To coat in sugar, spear each piece of fruit and plunge into boiling water, then roll in granulated sugar. To dip into syrup, place the remaining sugar and ¾ cup water in a saucepan. Heat gently until the sugar has dissolved, then boil for 1 minute. Dip each piece of fruit in boiling water, then quickly in the syrup. Place on the wire rack and let sit in a warm place until dry. Place the fruits in fluted candy papers and pack in boxes.

Fruit Fondant Chocolates

These chocolates are simple to make using plastic molds, yet they look very professional.

Fruit fondant is available at specialty-food stores and comes in a variety of flavors, including coffee and

nut. Try a mixture of flavors, using a small quantity of each, or use just a single flavor.

INGREDIENTS

8 squares semisweet,
milk or white chocolate
1 cup real fruit liquid fondant
3–4 teaspoons cooled boiled water

Decoration
1 tablespoon melted semisweet, milk or
white chocolate

Makes 24

1 Melt the chocolate. Use a piece of paper towel to polish the insides of the chocolate molds, to make sure that they are spotlessly clean. Fill up the shapes in one plastic tray to the top, let sit for a few seconds, then invert the tray over the bowl of melted chocolate, letting the excess chocolate fall back into the bowl. Sit the tray on the work surface and draw a spatula across the top to remove the excess chocolate and to neaten the edges. Chill until set. Repeat to fill the remaining trays.

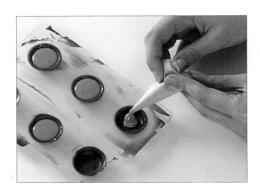

2 Sift the fruit fondant mixture into a bowl. Gradually stir in enough water to give it the consistency of thick cream. Place the fondant in a waxed-paper piping bag, fold down the top and snip off the end. Pipe in the fondant to fill each chocolate shell almost to the top. Let sit for 30 minutes, or until a skin has formed on the surface of the fondant.

3 Spoon the remaining melted chocolate over the fondant to fill each mold level to the top. Chill until the chocolate has set hard. Invert the tray and press out the chocolates one by one. Place melted chocolate of a contrasting color in a waxed paper piping bag, fold down the top, snip off the point and pipe lines across the top of each chocolate. Let set, then pack the chocolates in pretty boxes and tie with ribbon.

CHOCOLATE TRUFFLES

These truffles are a Christmas specialty in France.

They can be rolled in cocoa or nuts, or dipped in chocolate.

INGREDIENTS

¾ cup heavy cream
10 ounces semisweet chocolate, chopped
2 tablespoons unsalted butter,
cut into pieces
2–3 tablespoons brandy (optional)

For the Coating
cocoa powder
finely chopped pistachios or hazelnuts
14 ounces semisweet, milk or white
chocolate

Makes 20–30

1 Bring the cream to a boil. Remove from the heat and add the chocolate, then stir until melted. Stir in the butter and the brandy, if using, then strain into a bowl and cool. Cover and chill overnight.

2 Line a large baking sheet with waxed paper. Using two teaspoons, form the chocolate mixture into 20–30 balls and place on the paper. Chill if the mixture becomes soft.

3 To coat the truffles with cocoa, sift the cocoa into a bowl, drop in the truffles one at a time, and roll to coat well, keeping the round shape. To coat with nuts, roll truffles in finely chopped nuts. Chill, wrapped, for up to 10 days.

4 To coat the truffles with chocolate, freeze the truffles for at least 1 hour. In a small bowl, melt the semisweet, milk or white chocolate over a saucepan of barely simmering water, stirring until the chocolate has melted and is smooth, then let cool slightly.

5 Using a fork, dip the frozen truffles into the cooled chocolate, one at a time, tapping the fork on the edge of the bowl to shake off the excess. Place on a baking sheet lined with parchment paper and chill immediately. If the melted chocolate thickens, reheat until smooth. Wrap in plastic wrap and store in a cool place for up to 10 days.

MARSHMALLOWS

These light and fragrant mouthfuls of pale pink mousse are flavored with rosewater.

INGREDIENTS

oil, for greasing
3 tablespoons confectioners' sugar
3 tablespoons cornstarch
¼ cup cold water
3 tablespoons rosewater
1 envelope (1 tablespoon) powdered gelatin
pink food coloring
2 cups granulated sugar
2 level tablespoons liquid glucose
1 cup boiling water
2 egg whites

Makes 1¼ pounds

1 Lightly oil an 11 x 7-inch jelly-roll pan. Sift together the confectioners' sugar and cornstarch and use some to coat the inside of the pan.

2 Mix the cold water, rosewater, gelatin and a drop of food coloring in a bowl. Place over a pan of hot water. Stir until the gelatin has dissolved.

3 Place the granulated sugar, liquid glucose and boiling water in a heavy saucepan. Stir to dissolve the sugar.

4 Bring the syrup to a boil and boil steadily without stirring until the temperature reaches 260°F on a candy thermometer. Remove from the heat and stir in the gelatin mixture.

5 While the syrup is boiling, whisk the egg whites until stiff in a large bowl using an electric mixer. Pour a steady stream of syrup onto the egg whites while whisking continuously for about 3 minutes, until the mixture is thick and foamy. At this stage add more food coloring if the mixture looks too pale.

6 Pour the mixture into the prepared pan and let it set for about 4 hours or overnight. Sift some of the confectioners' sugar mixture over the surface of the marshmallow and the rest over a board or baking sheet. Ease the mixture away from the pan using an oiled spatula and invert onto the board. Cut into 1-inch squares, coating the cut sides with the confectioners' sugar mixture. Pack the marshmallows into glass containers or tins and seal well.

MARZIPAN FRUITS

These eye-catching and realistic fruits will make a perfect gift for lovers of marzipan.

INGREDIENTS

1 pound marzipan
yellow, green, red, orange and burgundy
food coloring dusts
2 tablespoons whole cloves

Makes 1 pound

1 Cover a baking sheet with baking parchment. Cut the marzipan into quarters. Take 1 piece and cut it into 10 even-size pieces. Place a little of each of the food coloring dusts into a clean palette, or place small amounts spaced apart on a plate. Cut two-thirds of the cloves into 2 pieces, making a stem and core end.

2 Shape the 10 marzipan pieces into neat balls. Dip 1 ball into the yellow food coloring and roll to color. Dip into the green coloring and roll to tint a green-yellow color. Roll one end to make a pear shape. Press a clove stem into the top and a core end into the base. Repeat with the remaining balls. Place on the prepared baking sheet.

3 Cut another piece of the marzipan into 10 pieces and shape into neat balls. Dip each piece of marzipan into the green food coloring dust and roll in the palms to color evenly. Add a spot of red coloring dust and roll gently to blend the color. Using a ball tool or the end of a fine paintbrush, indent the top and base to make an apple shape. Make a stem and core, using cloves.

4 Repeat as above, using another piece of the marzipan to make 10 orange-colored balls. Roll each over the surface of a fine grater to give the texture of an orange skin. Press a clove core into the base of each.

5 Take the remaining piece of marzipan, reserve a small piece, and mold the rest into lots of tiny beads. Color them burgundy with the food coloring. Place a clove on the baking sheet to make a stem. Arrange a cluster of burgundy beads in the shape of a bunch of grapes. Repeat with the remaining burgundy beads of marzipan to make another 3 bunches of grapes.

6 Roll out the remaining piece of marzipan thinly and brush with green food coloring. Using a vine leaf cutter, cut out 8 leaves, mark the veins with a knife and place 2 on each bunch of grapes. Let the fruits dry, then pack into gift boxes.

Peppermint Chocolate Sticks

These delicious bite-size chocolate sticks will prove irresistible.

INGREDIENTS

½ cup granulated sugar
⅔ cup water
½ teaspoon peppermint extract
7 ounces bittersweet chocolate, broken into squares
¼ cup toasted coconut

Makes about 80

1 Lightly oil a large baking sheet. Place the sugar and water in a small heavy saucepan over medium-low heat. Allow the water to heat gently until the sugar has dissolved completely. Stir occasionally.

2 Bring to a boil and boil rapidly until the syrup registers 280°F on a candy thermometer. Remove from the heat. Add the peppermint extract and pour onto the greased baking sheet. Let set.

3 Break up the peppermint mixture into a small bowl and use the end of a rolling pin to crush it into small pieces.

4 Melt the chocolate in a heatproof bowl over hot water. Remove from the heat and stir in the peppermint pieces and toasted coconut.

5 Spread the chocolate mixture over a 12 x 10-inch sheet of baking parchment to make a rectangle measuring about 10 x 8 inches. Let set. When firm, use a sharp knife to cut into thin sticks, each about 2½ inches long.

TRUFFLE CHRISTMAS PUDDINGS

Truffles disguised as Christmas puddings are great fun both to make and receive.

Make any flavor truffles, and decorate them as desired.

INGREDIENTS

20 plain chocolate truffles
1 tablespoon cocoa
1 tablespoon confectioners' sugar
1 cup white chocolate chips, melted
¼ cup white marzipan
green and red food colorings
yellow food coloring dust

Makes 20

2 Spread two-thirds of the white chocolate over a piece of baking parchment. Using a daisy cutter, stamp out 20 rounds. Place a truffle on the center of each shape, secured with reserved melted chocolate.

3 Color two-thirds of the marzipan green and one-third red. Roll out the green marzipan thinly and stamp out 40 leaves using a tiny holly leaf cutter. Mark the veins with a sharp knife. Mold lots of tiny red marzipan beads. Color the remaining white chocolate with yellow food coloring dust and place in a waxed-paper piping bag. Fold down the top of the bag, cut off the point and pipe the marzipan over the top of each truffle to resemble custard. Arrange the holly leaves and berries on the top of the puddings. When the truffle puddings have set, arrange them in gift boxes, label and tie with ribbon.

COOK'S TIP

These little truffle puddings are fun to make at home, and children will love to help. They may be able to coat the truffles, do some stamping, or pack the finished puddings in a box as a special present.

1 Make the truffles following the recipe on page 227. Sift the cocoa and confectioners' sugar together and coat the truffles.

Striped Cookies

Eat these cookies with scoops of vanilla ice cream or any light desserts.

INGREDIENTS

1 square (1 ounce) white chocolate, melted
red and green food coloring dusts
2 egg whites
⅓ cup superfine sugar
½ cup flour
4 tablespoons (½ stick) butter, melted

Makes 25

1 Preheat the oven to 375°F. Line two baking sheets with baking parchment. Divide the melted chocolate in half and use the food coloring dust to color the chocolate red and green. Fill two waxed-paper piping bags with each color chocolate and fold down the tops. Snip off the points.

2 Place the egg whites in a mixing bowl and whisk until they form stiff peaks. Gradually add the sugar to the bowl, whisking well after each addition, to make a thick meringue. Sift in the flour and melted butter and whisk some more until the mixture is smooth.

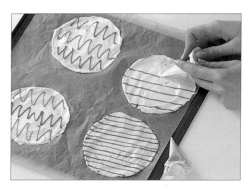

3 Drop 4 separate teaspoonfuls of mixture onto the baking sheets and spread into thin rounds. Pipe lines or zigzags of green and red chocolate over each round. Bake for 3–4 minutes, or until pale golden in color. Loosen the rounds with a spatula and return to the oven for a few seconds to soften. Have ready 2 or 3 wooden spoons, handles lightly oiled.

4 Taking one cookie out of the oven at a time, roll it around a spoon handle and set it aside for a few seconds to set. Repeat to shape the remaining cookies.

5 When the cookies are set, transfer to a wire rack to cool. Repeat with the remaining mixture and the red and green chocolate until all the mixture has been used.

6 When the cookies are cool, tie them together with a length of brightly colored ribbon and pack into airtight boxes, tins or glass jars.

ℳACAROONS

These little macaroons can be served as petits fours with coffee.

Dust with confectioners' sugar or cocoa before serving.

INGREDIENTS

⅔ cup ground almonds
¼ cup superfine sugar
1 tablespoon cornstarch
¼–½ teaspoon almond extract
1 egg white, whisked
15 whole almonds
4 candied cherries, quartered
confectioners' sugar or cocoa, to dust

Makes 30

2 Stir in just enough egg white to form a soft piping consistency. Place the mixture in a plastic piping bag fitted with a ½-inch plain piping nozzle.

3 Pipe about 15 rounds of mixture onto each baking sheet, spaced well apart. Press an almond onto half the macaroons and candied cherries onto the remainder. Bake for 10–15 minutes.

COOK'S TIP

To make chocolate-flavored macaroons, replace the cornstarch with the same amount of cocoa.

1 Preheat the oven to 325°F. Line two baking sheets with baking parchment. Place the ground almonds, sugar, cornstarch and almond extract into a bowl and combine well, using a wooden spoon.

INDIVIDUAL DUNDEE CAKES

Dundee cakes are traditionally topped with almonds but also look tempting covered with candied fruits.

INGREDIENTS

1 cup raisins
1 cup currants
1 cup golden raisins
¼ cup sliced candied cherries
¾ cup mixed citrus peel
grated rind of 1 orange
2¾ cups flour
½ teaspoon baking powder
1 teaspoon pumpkin pie spice
½ pound (2 sticks) unsalted butter, softened
1 cup superfine sugar
5 eggs

Topping
½ cup whole blanched almonds
¼ cup halved candied cherries
½ cup sliced candied fruits
3 tablespoons apricot glaze

Makes 3

1 Preheat the oven to 300°F. Grease and line three 6-inch round cake pans. Place all the fruit and the orange rind into a large mixing bowl. Combine until blended. In another bowl, sift the flour, baking powder and pumpkin pie spice. Add the butter, sugar and eggs. Combine and beat for 2–3 minutes, until smooth and glossy. Alternatively, use an electric mixer or a food processor for 1 minute.

2 Add the mixed fruit to the cake batter and fold in, using a spatula, until blended. Divide the cake mixture among the three pans and level the tops. Arrange the almonds in circles over the top of one cake, the candied cherries over the second cake and the mixed candied fruits over the last one. Bake for approximately 2–2½ hours, or until a skewer inserted into the center of the cakes comes out clean.

3 Let the cakes sit in their pans until completely cool. Turn out, remove the paper and brush the tops with apricot glaze. Let set, then wrap in cellophane or plastic wrap and place in pretty boxes.

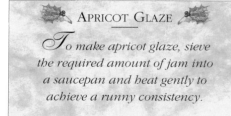

APRICOT GLAZE

To make apricot glaze, sieve the required amount of jam into a saucepan and heat gently to achieve a runny consistency.

Mini Black Buns

This is a traditional Scottish recipe, with a rich fruit cake mixture cooked inside a bun dough.

INGREDIENTS

4 tablespoons (½ stick) butter, melted, plus
extra for brushing
1 cup mixed dried fruit
¼ cup candied cherries, chopped
½ cup chopped almonds
2 teaspoons grated lemon rind
2 tablespoons superfine sugar
1 tablespoon whiskey
½ cup flour
1 teaspoon pumpkin pie spice
1 egg, beaten

Decoration
2 tablespoons apricot glaze
1 pound marzipan
purple and green food coloring

Makes 4

1 Preheat the oven to 300°F. Cut out four 6-inch squares of waxed paper and four squares of foil. Place the waxed-paper squares on top of the foil squares and brush with a little melted butter.

2 Place the dried fruit, chopped candied cherries, chopped almonds, lemon rind, superfine sugar, whiskey, sifted flour and pumpkin pie spice in a large mixing bowl. Using a wooden spoon, stir until all of the ingredients are well mixed. Add the melted butter and egg and beat until the mixture is well blended.

3 Divide the mixture among the four paper-and-foil squares, draw up the edges to the center of the foil and twist the squares to mold the mixture into rounds. Place on a baking sheet and bake for 45 minutes, until the mixture feels firm when touched. Remove the foil and bake for another 15 minutes. Open the paper and let the cakes cool on a wire rack.

4 Remove the paper and brush each cake with apricot glaze. Cut off one-fourth of the marzipan for decoration and put to one side. Cut the remainder into four pieces.

5 Roll out each piece of marzipan thinly and cover the cakes. Roll each cake in the palm of your hands to make them into round shapes. Prepare a hot broiler and place the cakes on a baking sheet lined with foil.

6 Broil the cakes until the marzipan is evenly browned. Let sit until cool. Color half of the remaining marzipan purple and half green. Cut out four purple thistle shapes, green leaves and stems and arrange them on top of each cake, moistening with a little water to stick. Wrap in cellophane and place in small cake boxes.

FLAVORED VINEGARS

Flavored vinegars look extra special if you pour them into beautifully shaped bottles.

INGREDIENTS

*good quality white and red wine vinegar
or cider vinegar*

Herb Vinegar
*1 tablespoon mixed peppercorns
2 lemon slices
4 garlic cloves
rosemary, thyme, tarragon and curry
plant sprigs*

Spice Vinegar
*1 tablespoon allspice berries
2 blades mace
2 teaspoons star anise
2 cinnamon sticks
1 orange*

Fruit Vinegar
*3 cups raspberries
3 cups blueberries
3 cups blackberries*

Makes 2½ cups
of each flavor

1 Sterilize two bottles with corks or caps. To the first bottle add the peppercorns, lemon slices and garlic cloves. Place the herb sprigs together and trim the stems so they vary in length. Insert them into the bottle, placing the short ones in first.

2 To the second bottle add the allspice berries, mace, star anise and cinnamon sticks. Cut two slices from the orange and insert into the bottle. Pare the rind from the remaining orange and insert into the bottle.

3 Using white wine vinegar, fill the bottle containing the herbs up to the neck. Repeat to fill the bottle containing the spices with red wine vinegar. Cork or cap the bottles and store them in a cool place.

4 Wash the raspberries, blueberries and blackberries separately under cold running water and place them in separate bowls. Crush the fruit with a wooden spoon.

5 Pour fruit into a separate clean wide-necked jar and add 2½ cups of white wine vinegar. Cover the jars and let sit for three to four days in a cool place. Shake the jars occasionally to mix well.

6 Strain fruit separately through a jelly bag or a cheesecloth-lined sieve into a stainless-steel saucepan and boil for 10 minutes. Pour into sterilized bottles or jars and seal with lids or tops with plastic-coated linings. All the vinegars should be used within 6 months.

BELL PEPPERS IN OLIVE OIL

The wonderful flavor and color of these peppers will add a Mediterranean

theme to festive meals. Bottle the peppers separately or mix the colors together.

INGREDIENTS

3 red bell peppers
3 yellow bell peppers
3 green bell peppers
1¼ cups olive oil
½ teaspoon salt
½ teaspoon freshly ground black pepper
3 thyme sprigs

Makes 3 pints

COOK'S TIP

This pungent oil should be stored in a cool, dark place and used within a week. The filled bottles also make great decorations for the home, if you choose not to use the oil for cooking.

2 Let the peppers cool for at least 5 minutes, then peel off the skins. Remove the cores, seeds and stalks. Slice each of the peppers thinly, keeping each color separate, and place each in a separate dish.

3 Pour one-third of the olive oil over each of the peppers. Season and add a sprig of thyme. Stir well. Sterilize three jars and lids and fill each with peppers. Fill up each jar with the oil. Screw the jar lids on firmly and label.

1 Prepare a hot broiler or preheat the oven to 400°F. Put the whole peppers on a broiler pan or a baking sheet. Place under the broiler or in the oven and cook for about 10 minutes, until the skins are charred and blistered all over. Turn the peppers frequently during the cooking time.

FRESH FRUIT PRESERVES

The wonderfully fresh flavor of this fruit spread makes it a welcome gift. To vary the recipe,

use a mixture of soft fruits or other individual fruits such as strawberries or blackberries.

INGREDIENTS
3½ cups raspberries
4 cups superfine sugar
2 tablespoons lemon juice
½ cup liquid pectin

Makes 2 pounds

COOK'S TIP

The process of leaving the fruit in the sugar for an hour is known as macerating. This process lets the fruit become very pulpy and sweet, with a more intense flavor.

1 Place the raspberries in a bowl and lightly crush with a wooden spoon. Stir in the superfine sugar. Let sit for 1 hour at room temperature, giving the mixture an occasional stir to dissolve the sugar.

2 Sterilize several small jars or containers and their lids, if being used. Add the lemon juice and liquid pectin to the raspberries and stir until thoroughly blended.

3 Spoon the raspberry mixture into the jars, leaving a ½-inch space at the top if the preserves are to be frozen. Cover the surface of each jar of preserves with a waxed paper disk, and cover with the jar lid or with cellophane and an elastic band. Do not use a screw-top lid if the preserves are to be frozen. Let cool, then label. The preserves can be stored in the freezer for up to 6 months, or refrigerated for up to 4 weeks.

FRUITS IN LIQUEURS

These eye-catching fruits in liqueurs are best made when the fruits are plentiful, cheap and in season.

Choose from apricots, clementines, kumquats, Cape gooseberries, cherries, raspberries, peaches, plums or

seedless grapes, and team them with rum, brandy, kirsch or Cointreau, to name just a few possibilities.

INGREDIENTS

3 cups fresh fruit
1 cup granulated sugar
⅔ cup liqueur or spirits

Makes 1 pound

1 Wash the fruit, halve and pit apricots, plums or peaches. Peel back and remove the husks from gooseberries, Hull strawberries, and prick kumquats, cherries or grapes all over with a toothpick. Pare the rind from clementines using a sharp knife, taking care not to leave any of the bitter white pith.

2 Place ½ cup of the sugar and 1¼ cups of water in a large saucepan. Heat gently, stirring occasionally, until the sugar has dissolved. Bring to a boil.

3 Add the fruit to the syrup and simmer gently for 1–2 minutes, until the fruit is just tender but the skins are still intact and the fruits are whole.

4 Carefully remove the fruit using a slotted spoon and arrange neatly in warmed sterilized jars. Add the remaining sugar to the syrup in the saucepan and stir continuously until it has dissolved.

5 Boil the syrup rapidly until it reaches 225°F, or the thread stage. Test by pressing a small amount of syrup between 2 teaspoons; when they are pulled apart, a thread should form. Let cool.

6 Measure the cooled syrup, then add an equal quantity of liqueur. Mix until blended. Pour over the fruit in the jars until covered. Seal each jar with a screw or clip top, label and keep for up to four months.

Festive Drinks & Cocktails

The cheerful custom of the Christmas "wassail"—
a steaming bowl of ale mixed with roasted apples, sugar
and spices—has existed for centuries as a celebration of
good cheer. The modern equivalent to this traditional toast
is the ever-popular Mulled Claret, and there are plenty of
other tempting alcoholic and non-alcoholic alternatives
included in this chapter. Brandied Eggnog is one of the
more warming recipes to lift the spirits and, along with
Irish Chocolate Velvet, makes the ultimate nightcap.
Cocktails such as Buck's Fizz and Cranberry Kiss
are perfect to get the party started, while for the post-party
breakfast, choose the delightful, sparkling Cranberry Frost.

CRANBERRY FROST

A nonalcoholic cocktail with the color of holly berries will delight younger and older guests alike.

It is the perfect one-for-the-road drink to serve at the end of a gathering.

INGREDIENTS

½ cup superfine sugar
juice of 2 oranges
still water, enough to dissolve the sugar
½ cup cranberry juice
4 cups sparkling mineral water
fresh cranberries, to decorate
sprigs of mint, to decorate

Serves 10

1 Put the sugar, juice and still water in a pan and stir over low heat to dissolve the sugar. Bring to a boil and boil for 3 minutes. Cool. The syrup can be made in advance and stored in a covered container in the refrigerator. Pour the syrup into a chilled bowl, pour on the cranberry juice and mix well. To serve, add to the sparkling water and decorate with cranberries and mint leaves.

COOK'S TIP

To make this fabulous nonalcoholic drink the very essence of festive color, chill with ice cubes made by freezing fresh red cranberries and tiny mint leaves in the water.

MULLED CLARET

This mull is a blend of claret, cider and orange juice. It can be varied to suit the occasion

by increasing or decreasing the proportion of fruit juice or, to give the mull more pep,

by adding up to two-thirds of a cup of brandy.

INGREDIENTS

1 orange
5 tablespoons honey
2 tablespoons raisins
2 clementines
a few cloves
whole nutmeg
¼ cup light brown sugar
2 cinnamon sticks
6 cups inexpensive claret
2½ cups medium cider
1¼ cups orange juice

Makes 16 ⅔-cup glasses

3 Grate a little nutmeg into the sugar and then add it to the pan with the cinnamon sticks. Pour in the wine and heat over low heat, stirring until the sugar has completely dissolved and the honey melted.

4 Pour the cider and the orange juice into the saucepan and continue to heat the mull over low heat. Do not let it boil, or all the alcohol will evaporate.

5 Warm a punch bowl or other large serving bowl. Remove the clementines and cinnamon sticks from the saucepan and strain the mull into the bowl to remove the raisins. Add the clementines studded with cloves, and serve the mull hot, in warmed glasses or in glasses containing a spoon (to prevent the glass from breaking). Using a nutmeg grater, grate a little nutmeg over each serving, if desired.

1 With a knife or a vegetable peeler, pare off a long strip of orange peel.

2 Place the orange peel, honey and raisins in a large pan. Stud the clementines all over with the cloves and add them to the saucepan.

BRANDIED EGGNOG

This frothy blend of eggs, milk and spirits definitely falls under the nightcap category of drinks.

INGREDIENTS

4 eggs, separated
2 tablespoons superfine sugar
¼ cup dark rum
¼ cup brandy
1¼ cups milk (or according to the
volume of the glasses), hot
whole nutmeg

Serves 4

1 Beat the egg yolks with the sugar. Beat the whites to soft peaks. Mix and pour into four heatproof glasses.

2 Pour in the rum and brandy, 1 tablespoon of each in each glass.

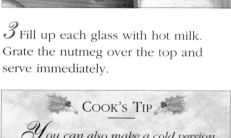

3 Fill up each glass with hot milk. Grate the nutmeg over the top and serve immediately.

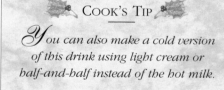

COOK'S TIP

You can also make a cold version of this drink using light cream or half-and-half instead of the hot milk.

Irish Chocolate Velvet

This smooth, sophisticated drink will always be appreciated on cold Christmas evenings.

INGREDIENTS

½ cup heavy cream
1⅔ cups milk
2 tablespoons cocoa
4 ounces milk chocolate, broken into squares
¼ cup Irish whiskey
whipped cream, for topping
chocolate curls, to decorate

Serves 4

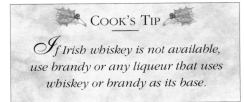

COOK'S TIP

If Irish whiskey is not available, use brandy or any liqueur that uses whiskey or brandy as its base.

1 Whip the cream in a bowl until it is thick enough to hold its shape.

2 Put the milk in a saucepan and whisk in the cocoa. Add the chocolate squares and heat gently, stirring, until the chocolate has melted. Bring the chocolate milk to a boil.

3 Remove the saucepan from the heat and add the whipped heavy cream and Irish whiskey. Stir gently for about 1 minute to blend well.

4 Pour quickly into four heatproof mugs or glasses and top each serving with a generous spoonful of whipped cream. Decorate with chocolate curls and serve immediately.

Buck's Fizz (Mimosa)

This delightfully refreshing drink, invented by the barman at the Buck's Club in

London in 1921, has achieved star status. In France it is known as Champagne-orange,

and in Italy and the United States as a Mimosa.

INGREDIENTS

½ cup fresh orange juice
1 teaspoon grenadine syrup
¾ cup champagne or other sparkling white wine, chilled

Makes 1 glass

1 Put the orange juice in a chilled long-stemmed glass. Add the grenadine and stir with a long-handled spoon to blend. Then add the champagne and stir again. Serve the cocktail immediately, decorated with a slice of fresh orange.

COOK'S TIP

Buck's Fizz, with its refreshing combination of fruit juice and champagne, makes the perfect cocktail drink for Christmas morning.

Brandy Alexander

A warming digestif, made from a blend of crème de cacao, brandy and heavy cream,

that can be served at the end of the meal with coffee.

Ingredients

crushed ice
1½ tablespoons brandy
1½ tablespoons crème de cacao
1½ tablespoons heavy cream
whole nutmeg, grated, to decorate

Serves 1

3 Strain the chilled cocktail into a small wineglass.

4 Grate a little nutmeg over the top of the cocktail and serve immediately..

Variation

*W*arm the brandy and heavy cream and whip in a blender with crème de cacao until frothy. Serve in a tall glass with a cinnamon stick.

1 Half fill the cocktail shaker with ice and pour in the brandy, crème de cacao and, finally, the cream.

2 Ensure that the lid is screwed firmly in place and shake for about 20 seconds to combine the ingredients well.

CRANBERRY KISS

A delicious full-flavored cocktail, with the tang of cranberry and pink

grapefruit juices and the sweetness of Marsala.

INGREDIENTS

red currants, to decorate
1 egg white, lightly beaten, to decorate
¼ cup superfine sugar, to decorate
crushed ice
3 tablespoons cranberry juice
1½ tablespoons brandy
3 tablespoons pink grapefruit juice
3 tablespoons marsala

Serves 1

1 Lightly brush the red currants with the egg white.

2 Shake superfine sugar over the red currants, to cover them in a light frosting. Set them aside to dry.

3 Place the cranberry juice with the brandy and grapefruit juice in a cocktail shaker full of crushed ice and shake for 20 seconds to mix thoroughly.

4 Strain the cocktail mixture into a well-chilled glass.

5 Tilt the glass slightly before slowly pouring the marsala down the side of the glass into the drink.

6 Serve the cocktail decorated with the frosted red currants.

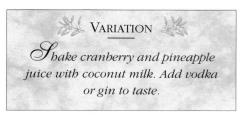

VARIATION

Shake cranberry and pineapple juice with coconut milk. Add vodka or gin to taste.

Fruit and Ginger Ale

An old English mulled drink, served chilled over ice. It can be made with

purchased apple and orange juices, but roasting the fruit with cloves gives a far superior flavor.

INGREDIENTS

1 apple
1 orange, scrubbed
1 lemon, scrubbed
20 whole cloves
3-inch piece fresh ginger, peeled
1½ tablespoons brown sugar
1½ cups bitter lemon or nonalcoholic wine
wedges of orange rind and whole cloves,
to decorate

Serves 4–6

3 Add 1¼ cups boiling water. Using a spoon, squeeze the fruit to release more flavor. Cover the mixing bowl and let cool for several hours or overnight.

4 Strain into a pitcher full of cracked ice and use a spoon to press out all the juices from the fruit. Add the bitter lemon or nonalcoholic wine to taste. Decorate with orange rind and cloves.

1 Preheat the oven to 400°F. Score the apple around the middle and stud the orange and lemon with the cloves. Bake them for 25 minutes, until soft and cooked.

2 Quarter the orange and lemon and pulp the apple, discarding the skin and the core. Finely grate the ginger. Place the fruit and ginger in a bowl with the brown sugar.

CHRISTMAS SPIRIT

This colorful drink has a sharp but sweet taste. It is excellent served as a winter warmer

or after a meal, but it also makes a good summer drink served with crushed ice.

INGREDIENTS

2 cups cranberries
2 clementines
2 cups granulated sugar
1 cinnamon stick
2 cups vodka

Makes 3 cups

1 Crush the cranberries in a food processor and spoon into a large jar. Pare the rind from the clementines and add.

2 Squeeze the juice from the clementines and add to the cranberries and pared rind in the jar. Add the sugar, cinnamon stick and vodka to the jar and seal with the lid or a double thickness of plastic, and tie down securely. Shake the jar well to combine all the ingredients.

3 Store the jar in a cool place for one month, shaking the jar daily for two weeks, then occasionally. When the drink has matured, sterilize some small pretty bottles and, using a funnel with a filter paper inside, strain the liquid into the bottles and cork immediately. Label the bottles clearly and tie gift tags around their necks.

COOK'S TIP

Sterilize the storage containers you are using with a campden tablet dissolved in boiling water.

Festive Liqueurs

These are easier to make than wines and may be made with a variety of flavors and spirits.

All these liqueurs should mature for three months before drinking.

INGREDIENTS

Plum Brandy
1 pound plums
1 cup light brown sugar
2½ cups brandy

Fruit Gin
3 cups raspberries or
black currants
1½ cups granulated sugar
3 cups gin

Citrus Whiskey
1 large orange
1 small lemon
1 lime
1 cup granulated sugar
2½ cups whiskey

Makes 3¾ cups of each liqueur

1 Sterilize three jars and lids. Wash and halve the plums, remove the pits and slice. Place the plums in the sterilized jar with the sugar and brandy. Crack three of the plum pits, remove the kernels and chop. Add them to the jar and stir until blended.

2 Place the raspberries or black currants in the prepared jar. Add the sugar and gin to the jar and stir until the mixture is well blended.

3 To make the Citrus Whiskey, first scrub the fruit. Using a sharp knife or potato peeler, pare the rind from the fruit, taking care not to include the white pith. Squeeze out all of the juice and place in the jar with the fruit rinds. Add the sugar and whiskey, and stir until well blended.

4 Cover the jars with lids or double-thick pieces of plastic wrap tied down well. Store the jars in a cool, dark place for three months.

5 Shake the Fruit Gin every day for 1 month, and occasionally thereafter. Shake the Plum Brandy and Citrus Whiskey every day for 2 weeks, then occasionally. Sterilize the chosen bottles and corks or stoppers for each liqueur.

6 When each liqueur is ready to be bottled, strain the liquid through a sieve, then pour it into sterilized bottles through a funnel with a filter paper. Put in the corks or stoppers and label the bottles with festive labels.

Suggested Menus

Christmas Dinner
for 8 People

Roquefort Tartlets

*Roast Turkey, stuffing balls, sausages,
bacon rolls and gravy*

Festive Brussels Sprouts

Traditional Christmas Pudding

Vegetarian Christmas Dinner
for 8 People

Christmas Salad with rolls

Cheese and Spinach Tart or Vegetarian Christmas Pie

Garden Vegetable Terrine or Festive Brussels Sprouts

Crunchy Apple and Almond Tart

Boxing Day Lunch
for 12 People

Warm Shrimp Salad with herb-and-garlic bread

Baked Ham with Cumberland Sauce

Vegetable Gnocchi

Deluxe Mincemeat Tart

HOT FORK SUPPER
for 12 People

Roquefort Tartlets and Filo Vegetable Pie

Chicken with Red Wine Vinegar

Sweet-and-Sour Red Cabbage

Iced Praline Torte and Ruby Fruit Salad

COLD BUFFET LUNCH
for 12 People

Layered Salmon Terrine

Fillet of Beef with Ratatouille

Turkey Rice Salad

*Ginger Trifle and Almond
Mincemeat Tartlets*

NEW YEAR'S EVE PARTY
for 8 People

Smoked Salmon Salad

Roast Goose with Caramelized Apples

Gratin Dauphinois and Sweet-and-Sour Red Cabbage

Chocolate and Chestnut Yule Log

INDEX

A

Advent candle ring, 9
almonds: almond paste, 12
  amaretti, 214
  iced praline torte, 180
  macaroons, 233
  tapas of olives, cheese and, 122
amaretti, 214
Amaretto mousses with Chocolate
  Sauce, 186
anchovy spread, 149
apples: apple and mint jelly, 155
  apple and nut stuffing, 36
  crab apple and lavender jelly, 154
  crunchy apple and almond tart, 170
  filo crackers, 134
apricots: apricot and orange stuffing,
  142
  apricot and raisin stuffing, 140
  golden ginger compote, 162
avocados: celery, avocado and walnut
  salad, 116
  guacamole, 124

B

beef: Chateaubriand with béarnaise
  sauce, 49
  filet mignon with mushrooms, 48
  fillet of beef with ratatouille, 98
  hot pastrami on a stick, 127
  roast beef with roasted bell
    peppers, 50
bell peppers: bell peppers in olive oil, 237
  roast beef with roasted bell
    peppers, 50
black buns, mini, 235
blinis with smoked salmon and dill
  cream, 131
brandy: brandied eggnog, 244
  brandy Alexander, 247
  plum brandy, 251
  poached spiced plums in brandy, 156
bread: bread sauce, 143
  stollen, 201
Brie and walnuts, broiled, 25
Brussels sprouts: festive, 78
  stir-fried Brussels sprouts, 85
Buck's fizz (mimosa), 246
bulghur and ham salad, 115
butter: Cumberland rum butter, 147
  savory butters, 148

C

cake pans, lining, 13
cakes: chocolate and chestnut Yule
    log, 176
  individual Dundee cakes, 234
  light jeweled fruit cake, 202
  mini black buns, 235
  moist and rich Christmas cake, 204
  nut and candied fruit ring, 199
  panettone, 200
  spiced Christmas cake, 203
candle ring, Advent, 9
candy, 222–30
caramel: iced praline torte, 180
carrots: carrot and coriander soup, 16
  carrot, apple and orange coleslaw,
    117
  glazed carrots with cider, 84
carving turkey, 12
celery, avocado and walnut salad, 116
champagne: buck's fizz (mimosa), 246
Chateaubriand with Béarnaise sauce, 49
cheese: broiled Brie and walnuts, 25
  cheese and spinach tart, 70
  cheese, rice and vegetable strudel, 66
  cheeselets, 120
  cocktail crackers, 121
  goat cheese soufflé, 24
  Parmesan filo triangles, 132
  Roquefort and cucumber mousse, 26
  Roquefort tartlets, 33
  sablés with goat cheese and
    strawberries, 136
  vegetable crumble with anchovies, 68
  vegetable gnocchi, 64
  vegetarian Christmas pie, 62
cheesecake, raspberry and white
  chocolate, 190
chestnuts: chestnut and mushroom
    loaf, 71
  chestnut stuffing, 140
chicken: chicken roll, 103
  chicken satay with peanut sauce, 129
  chicken with morels, 43
  chicken with red wine vinegar, 42
  farmhouse pâté, 31
chocolate: Amaretto mousses with
    chocolate sauce, 186
  chocolate and chestnut Yule log, 176
  chocolate crêpes with plums and
    port, 188
  chocolate, date and almond filo coil, 189

chocolate kisses, 211
chocolate roulade with coconut
    cream, 192
chocolate sorbet with red fruits, 184
chocolate truffles, 227
fruit fondant chocolates, 226
ginger Florentines, 210
Irish chocolate velvet, 245
mocha Viennese swirls, 215
orange, mint and coffee meringues,
    223
peppermint chocolate sticks, 230
raspberry and white chocolate
    cheesecake, 190
rich chocolate and fruit fondue, 137
tiramisù in chocolate cups, 179
truffle Christmas puddings, 231
chorizo puffs, pastry-wrapped, 126
Christmas cookies, 208
Christmas cakes, 203-4
Christmas chutney, 150
Christmas cranberry bombe, 183
Christmas pie, vegetarian, 62
Christmas pudding, Traditional, 174
Christmas salad, 22
Christmas spirit, 250
Christmas tree, everlasting, 9
chutneys, 150–2
cinnamon rolls, 213
citrus whiskey, 251
claret, mulled, 243
cocktail crackers, 121
coffee: mocha Viennese swirls, 215
  tiramisu in chocolate cups, 179
coleslaw, carrot, apple and orange, 117
consommé, Asian duck, 19
cookies: amaretti, 214
  cheeselets, 120
  chocolate kisses, 211
  Christmas cookies, 208
  cocktail cookies, 121
  festive gingerbread, 196
  ginger Florentines, 210
  macaroons, 233
  mocha Viennese swirls, 215
  New Year's shortbread, 207
  orange shortbread fingers, 206
  sablés with goat cheese and
    strawberries, 136
  striped cookies, 232
couscous, spiced vegetable, 72
crab apple and lavender jelly, 154

crackers, filo, 134
cranberries: Christmas cranberry
   bombe, 183
   Christmas spirit, 250
   cranberry and rice stuffing, 140
   cranberry frost, 242
   cranberry kiss, 248
   cranberry sauce, 143
crème Anglaise, 146
crêpes: chocolate, 188
   with orange sauce, 166
cucumber and Roquefort mousse, 26
Cumberland rum butter, 147
Cumberland sauce, baked ham
   with, 52
custard: baked custard with burnt
   sugar, 182
   crème Anglaise, 146

D
date-filled pastries, 212
drinks, 242–51
duck: duck with orange sauce, 44
   Asian duck consommé, 19
Dundee cakes, individual, 234

E
eggnog, brandied, 244
eggs: baked eggs with creamy leeks, 32
evergreen garland, 8

F
farmhouse pâté, 31
filo crackers, 134
filo vegetable pie, 74
foie gras in filo cups, 28
fondant icing, 13
fondue, rich chocolate and fruit, 137
fruit: Christmas chutney, 150
   candied fruits, 225
   fruit and ginger ale, 249
   fruit fondant chocolates, 226
   fruits in liqueurs, 239
   marzipan fruits, 229
   rich chocolate and fruit fondue, 137
   ruby fruit salad, 161
   sea bass with citrus fruit, 54
fudge, creamy, 222

G
game terrine, 94
garland, evergreen, 8

gin, fruit, 251
ginger: festive gingerbread, 196
   fruit and ginger ale, 249
   ginger Florentines, 210
   ginger trifle, 160
   gingerbread heart ring, 198
   golden ginger compote, 162
gnocchi, 64, 76
goat cheese soufflé, 24
goose, roast with caramelized
   apples, 36
gougère, vegetable, 65
Grand Marnier soufflés, frozen, 178
gratin Dauphinois, 88
green beans with bacon and
   cream, 87
guacamole, 124

H
ham and bulghur salad, 115
ham, baked with Cumberland
   sauce, 52
Hasselback potatoes, 91

I
ice cream: Christmas cranberry
   bombe, 183
iced praline torte, 180
icings, 13
Irish chocolate velvet, 245

J
jellies, 154–5

K
Koulibiac, 66
kumquats: golden ginger compote, 162

L
lamb: lamb tikka, 128
   roast stuffed lamb, 51
leeks: baked eggs with creamy
   leeks, 32
   leek and onion tart, 80
   mini leek and onion tartlets, 104
liqueurs: festive liqueurs, 251
   fruits in liqueurs, 239
liver: chicken liver mousse, 30
   farmhouse pâté, 31
lobster thermidor, 58

M
macaroons, 233
mango and amaretti strudel, 172
marshmallows, 228
marzipan fruits, 229
meringues, orange, mint and
   coffee, 223
millefeuille, mini, 168
mimosa, 246
mincemeat: almond mincemeat
   tartlets, 217
   deluxe mincemeat tart, 218
   double-crust mince pies, 216
mocha Viennese swirls, 215
mousseline sauce, 145
mousses: Amaretto, 186
   chicken liver, 30
   Roquefort and cucumber, 26
mulled claret, 243
mushrooms: chestnut and mushroom
   loaf, 71
   chicken with morels, 43
   cream of mushroom soup, 17
   filet mignon with mushrooms, 48
   vegetarian Christmas pie, 62
   wild mushroom polenta, 23
   wild mushroom tart, 100
mussels, sole with shrimp and, 56

N
New Year's shortbread, 207
nut and candied fruit ring, 199

O
onions: onion marmalade, 30
   thyme-roasted onions, 81
orange: Buck's fizz (mimosa), 246
   crêpes with orange sauce, 166
   duck with orange sauce, 44
   orange, mint and coffee meringues,
   223
   orange shortbread fingers, 206

P
panettone, 200
Parmesan filo triangles, 132
parsley, lemon and thyme stuffing, 142
parsnip and chestnut croquettes, 83
pâtés, 28, 31
peaches stuffed with mascarpone
   cream, 164
pears: spiced pears in red wine, 163

spiced pickled pears, 157
peas with baby onions and cream, 86
peppermint chocolate sticks, 230
pheasant: roast pheasant with port, 40
piccalilli, 151
pies: double-crust mince pies, 216
  filo vegetable pie, 74
  turkey and cranberry pie, 96
  vegetarian Christmas pie, 62
pilaf, smoked trout, 110
pizza wedges, spicy sun-dried tomato,
  130
plums: chocolate crêpes with, 188
  plum brandy, 251
  poached spiced plums in brandy, 156
pork: tenderloin wrapped in bacon, 53
potatoes: gratin Dauphinois, 88
  Hasselback potatoes, 91
  mini filled baked potatoes, 133
  sautéed potatoes, 90
praline: iced praline torte, 180
preserves, fresh fruit, 238
pumpkin: pumpkin gnocchi, 76
  pumpkin soup, 18

Q
quince paste, 153

R
raisin and nut stuffing, 142
raspberries: fresh fruit preserves, 238
  mini millefeuille, 168
  raspberry and white chocolate
    cheesecake, 190
ratatouille, fillet of beef with, 98
red cabbage, sweet-and-sour, 82
red currant jelly: baked ham with
  Cumberland sauce, 52
red fruit filo baskets, 169
rice: cheese, rice and vegetable
  strudel, 66
  cranberry and rice stuffing, 140
  smoked trout pilaf, 110
  turkey rice salad, 114
roasting times, turkey, 12
Roquefort and cucumber mousse, 26
Roquefort tartlets, 33
royal icing, 13
ruby fruit salad, 161
rum butter, Cumberland, 147

S
sablés with goat cheese and
  strawberries, 136
salads, 20–2, 114–17
salmon: classic whole salmon, 106
  layered salmon terrine, 108
  salmon steaks with sorrel sauce, 59
sauces: bread, 143
  cranberry, 143
  crème Anglai, 146
  mousseline, 145
  tartare, 144
sea bass with citrus fruit, 54
shortbread, 206–7
shrimp: shrimp toasts, 125
  sole with shrimp and mussels, 56
  warm shrimp salad with spicy
    marinade, 20
smoked salmon: blinis with dill cream
  and, 131
  smoked salmon salad, 21
smoked trout pilaf, 110
sole with shrimp and mussels, 56
sorbet, chocolate, 184
soufflés: frozen Grand Marnier, 178
  goat cheese, 24
soups, 16–19
spinach: cheese and spinach tart, 70
  creamy spinach purée, 79
  roast stuffed lamb, 51
  vegetable gnocchi, 64
stollen, 201
striped cookies, 232
strudels, 66, 172
stuffings: apple and nut, 36
  apricot and orange, 142
  apricot and raisin, 140
  chestnut, 140
  cranberry and rice, 140
  parsley, lemon and thyme, 142
  prune, 53
  raisin and nut, 142
sweet-and-sour red cabbage, 82

T
tapas of almonds, olives and cheese,
  122
tartare sauce, 144
tarts: almond mincemeat tartlets, 217
  cheese and spinach tart, 70
  crunchy apple and almond tart, 170
  deluxe mincemeat tart, 218

leek and onion tart, 80
  mini leek and onion tartlets, 104
  Roquefort tartlets, 33
  tomato and basil tart, 112
  wild mushroom tart, 100
terrines: game, 94
  garden vegetable, 102
  layered salmon, 108
tiramisù in chocolate cups, 179
tomatoes: spicy sun-dried tomato pizza
  wedges, 130
  tomato and basil tart, 112
  tomato chutney, 152
trifle, ginger, 160
trout, smoked see smoked trout
truffles: chocolate truffles, 227
  truffle Christmas puddings, 231
turkey: carving, 12
  roast turkey, 12, 38
  turkey and cranberry pie, 96
  turkey rice salad, 114
Turkish delight, 224
twig heart door wreath, 8

V
vegetables: cheese, rice and vegetable
  strudel, 66
  fillet of beef with ratatouille, 98
  filo vegetable pie, 74
  garden vegetable terrine, 102
  piccalilli, 151
  spiced vegetable couscous, 72
  vegetable crumble with anchovies, 68
  vegetable gnocchi, 64
  vegetable gougère, 65
vegetarian Christmas pie, 62
venison, roast leg of, 46
Viennese swirls, mocha, 215
vinegars, flavored, 236
vodka: Christmas spirit, 250

W
whiskey: citrus whiskey, 251
  Irish chocolate velvet, 245
wild mushroom tart, 100
wine: mulled claret, 243
  spiced pears in red wine, 163
wreath, twig heart door, 8

Y
Yule log, chocolate and chestnut, 176